TRICK TRAINING
FOR CATS

TRICK TRAINING FOR CATS

Smart fun with the clicker

by Christine Hauschild

Acknowledgements!

My special thanks go to the photographers Christina Boumala and Kai Nissen as well as the animal trainers Helena Dbalý and Christina Nissen for their dedicated cooperation and the marvellous photographs. Honour where honour is due goes to the photographic stars of this book: Birne, Cuno, Eazy, Faramir, Lütti, Plato and ZsaZsi.

The Gender Question

The 'she' pronoun has been used throughout the text. It is however not gender-specific and tomcats as well as queens are invited to join in the fun.

Dedicated to

Special Agent ZsaZsi and heroic Tomcat Eazy

Imprint

Copyright © 2011 Cadmos Publishing Ltd, Richmond Upon Thames, UK

Copyright of original edition © 2010 Cadmos Verlag GmbH, Schwarzenbek, Germany

Layout: jb:design – Johanna Böhm, Möhnsen

Translation: Konstanze Allsopp

Editorial: Anneke Bosse, Christopher Long

Cover photograph: JBTierfoto

Text photos: Christina Boumala, Kai Nissen, Elina Rüter

Printed by: Westermann Druck, Zwickau

British Library Cataloguing in Publication Data

A catalogue record of this book is available from the British Library.

Printed in Germany

ISBN 978-0-85788-400-8

(Photo: Nissen)

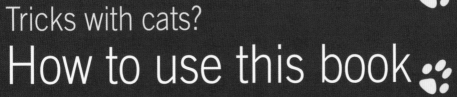

Tricks with cats?
How to use this book

In my opinion, clicker training is one of the most entertaining and rewarding things that a human being and his/her cat can do together. The aim is not to reduce the status of the cat to that of a subservient creature without any willpower of her own that jumps if we command her to 'jump'.

Clicker training encourages cats to be active, to try to explore new behaviour patterns and to improve their agility. It can help timid cats to gain more selfesteem, passive cats to develop more initiative, and impatient and unruly cats to improve their self-control. Most importantly, this type of training requires that your cat uses her mind and learns new things. It is therefore a great method to fight against chronic lack of challenges in the everyday environment of many housebound cats.

At the start of your trick training you will have two roles to fulfil. You are learning something completely new, but from the start you are also the trainer of your cat. It depends largely on your qualities as a trainer how easily and with what enjoyment your cat is able to learn the tricks. Clicker training is based on the voluntary cooperation of your cat, and you will succeed if your training is fun for your cat. This can depend on a multitude of small and large factors, therefore it is worthwhile if you familiarise yourself with these factors before you start your training.

I am sure that you have already had a browse through the pages of this book and have read one or the other trick instructions. At least, that is what I would have done in your place, and my fingers would be itching to start immediately with the first exercise! However, I would ask you to take some time with your preparation. Your cat will only be able to carry out trick training with success and enjoyment if you lead her through the exercises without hesitation and in a calm manner. You will only achieve this if you first acquire the necessary knowledge and do a bit of practical work as well. Don't worry; this is not a textbook! You will be able to start the training with your cat very soon.

You will find the instructions for the first tricks, together with further information regarding training techniques, from page 31 onwards. Please follow the exercises in this chapter with your cat in the given order, as they form the basis of all subsequent tricks and exercises. Following that, you will be able to teach your cat all the other tricks and ideas in this book. Initially you should practise clicking with a person; work on your timing and get some experience under your belt. If that works well, you will be able to show your cat the path to a variety of different tricks. Also, allow her a bit of time to learn what the principle of clicker training is about. You will recognise the moment when your cat has 'clicked' with what you want from her!

I wish you many wonderful moments, exciting discoveries and loads of fun during your clicker training!

Christine Hauschild, August 2010

(Photo: Boumala)

From click to trick

The tricks described in this book will be taught with the help of clicker training – a fascinating technique to make your cat understand what you expect from her. She will be motivated to carry out other actions by means of the clicker training.

The most important tool – the clicker

The most important training tool that you need is the clicker. It is the kind of cricket toy which makes a sharp, short sound when you press down on it. These days you can easily get a clicker either from a pet shop or on the Internet. They come in different forms and colours and – this aspect is important for your cat – in different volume levels. The quietest clicker that I know of is the so-called I-click, which was developed by the clicker pioneer Karen Pryor.

You can also employ other sounds as an alternative to the clicker, for example the clicking sound of a biro pen. However, whichever clicker you choose to use needs to fulfil two criteria: it should always sound the same, and it must not be a sound that the cat hears constantly outside the training sessions during her day-to-day experiences. Unless you click your tongue to call your cat or tell her that food is ready (which is something a lot of people do), I would recommend the tongue-clicking sound. Clicking with the tongue is well-suited as a clicking sound and offers two great advantages: you will have your hand free because you don't have to hold the clicker, and you can also click your tongue spontaneously outside training sessions.

Clicker training tools: different target sticks, selection of titbits, clicker hoop, small titbit can, and pouch. (Photo: Nissen)

Do you have problems clicking your tongue?

In this case, try to make a loud kissing sound – a real smacker – this creates a similar sound.

It is time for humans – the clicker game

It is time to proceed with the first practical exercise. However, in this first exercise you don't use the clicker on your cat. Instead, try it out with another person. Invite your partner, a friend or your child to play the clicking game – you can promise them a lot of fun without investing too much!

The clicker game works as follows: imagine an action that your game partner should carry out. Start with something simple: to sit on a specific chair; to touch the window handle; to touch the light switch. Do not tell your game partner what you expect from him/her, but ask them instead to figure out by themselves what you want them to do by trying out a number of different things. Use the clicker as a helpful aid. Explain to your partner that the click means: 'Great, you are on the right track' and that you will not speak to him/her in any other way, nor are you allowed to give them additional hints. You will point them towards the right goal solely by means of the clicker.

Touching the light switch, for example, could proceed as follows: your partner looks or moves in the direction of the light switch – click! He/she looks in another direction – no click. He/she looks roughly towards the light switch again – click! He/she moves a leg to step in the correct direction – click! Another step – click! However, if he/she moves past the light switch and through the door – no click. He/she asks: 'Shouldn't I go this way?' You smile in a gentle manner, don't say a word and wait for the next opportunity to click: he/she turns around – click! If he/she now walks past the light switch in the other direction –no click! He/she turns around again – click! He/she is now limited to the space near the door frame and touches it with his/her hand – click! He/she touches the door frame again at the height of the light switch – click! If he/she touches the doorframe much higher than the light switch – no click! He/she touches the doorframe again at the same height as the light switch – click! He/she moves his/her hand in the direction of the light switch – click! If he/she presses down the light switch – click and verbal confirmation: 'Great! That's exactly what I wanted!'

This sounds very easy but it requires a number of things from the trainer. To begin with you need to think in detail about what result you want to see at the end of the exercise. You should envisage in your mind which signs your game partner could offer on the way to the ultimate goal. That could mean a first step in the direction of the target object, but as a rule you will probably have to start with an earlier sign: a look at or a slight leaning forwards in the right direction. Unless you have defined these small steps for yourself

'Something to do with the drawer?' The light switch is already close but is yet to be recognised as the target object. (Photo: Nissen)

in advance, you will automatically start pondering over them during the game. 'Should I click this action now? One step is good, of course, but it wasn't completely in the right direction. Hmm, maybe I should have already clicked a moment ago, when he/she looked in that direction …'. While all these thoughts go around in your head, your game partner is not rewarded with a click. That isn't a very nice feeling, as in the first place your game partner does not get the expected confirmation that his/her action was right and secondly he/she will feel slightly helpless, a feeling which can restrict further activities and attempts. It is clear that a high level of clarity and the greatest degree of attention are needed in order that you don't miss even the slightest attempts and movements.

This ensures that your game partner will find the game easier and will experience a greater sense of motivation, if he/she is rewarded with a click as a result of an action on his/her part. In order for that to work, the clicker needs to be used at the exact moment of the action. For example, if you want your partner to walk several steps forward, you always need to click at the exact moment when he/she lifts a leg to step forward. If you are slightly late and use the clicker when your partner has placed his/her foot back on the ground, he/she will hesitate and stop, because you are signalling to him/her that he/she is supposed to have both legs firmly on the ground and should not step forwards any further.

Your game partner will be a marvellous indicator of your ability to use the clicker correctly. To begin with he/she will probably frequently complain, 'What do you want me to do now?' or 'I don't understand what you want me to do…'. You should make use of these complaints to analyse which things present difficulties for your game partner. The better you become, the less frequently these moments will occur, and your partner will perform certain behavioural patterns during the exercise with increasing speed and with greater enjoyment.

You should definitely swap places as well. You will experience what it feels like if the clicker isn't used at the precise moment of your action or is used infrequently, and feel how great it is when one click is followed closely by another and all your actions are confirmed in each case through the 'Correct!' click.

If possible, practise with a number of different people in order to become competent with various characters – every person and every cat has slightly different behavioural strategies which will become apparent in the clicker situation. Think of differing tasks and slowly increase their degree of difficulty. Have the last five of your clicker games been fluent, fun and successful? Did your game partners ask for more? If that is the case you can start practising with your cat. However, we need to make sure in advance that your cat understands what the click sound means.

The meaning of the click – a change from a simple sound to a great promise

At the moment, your cat hasn't got a clue. She doesn't know that she will soon experience a regular daily fun-filled work-out to liven up her boring day-to-day routine, and at this moment the click sound has absolutely no meaning for your cat. If she hears a click, she will probably look up for a moment to determine what kind of sound it is and will then continue to do what she was doing beforehand anyway.

We change that by associating the click with something very rewarding for the cat – or to be precise, with a titbit.

Step One: Conditioning your cat to understand the meaning of the click

Depending on the appetite of your cat, prepare between five and eight small treats. Take them in one hand and the clicker in the other and go and sit with your cat.

Press the clicker once and immediately give your cat a titbit. The precise order in which you do this is very important; first use the clicker, then give your cat the titbit. Wait for a moment and then click again and immediately give her another titbit.

The pause between the click sound and giving the cat a titbit should be less than a second. Continue this exercise until your cat has eaten up all the prepared titbits. Please don't expect anything spectacular. Your cat will be happy about the titbits, but at this stage she doesn't have to do anything to get them. In this way she learns very quickly that the click sound announces a titbit.

This learning process is called classical conditioning. From now on, the click sound is no longer a neutral, unimportant noise for your cat but instead announces the appearance of a titbit and thus gains a positive meaning – 'delicious!'

If your cat is still asking for more at this stage, you can start teaching the first trick immediately.

Classical conditioning occurs frequently, and usually unplanned, during the normal daily routine. Does your cat come running if you go to the cupboard where you keep her feed or open the fridge door? She has learned that this means – or could mean – that you are going to feed her. But it doesn't just concern the feeding routine alone.

My own cats react by welcoming me, by performing activities, or by suggesting that I play with them if I finish a telephone call or put down my book. The words and noises used in connection with any of these actions tell them that the chances of a round of games or cuddling are pretty good.

Plato is walking from one chair to the other to earn a click and a treat. (Photo: Boumala)

14

(See nose touching the target stick, page 25.) The combination of click-titbit will be strengthened further during the training process.

Suitable titbits

The effect of the clicking sound rises with the quality of the titbit rewards. Your cat alone decides which titbits are of high quality, namely fantastically delicious ones! Is there anything your cat would do just about anything for? This feed is exactly the right titbit to use during trick training with the clicker.

Small titbits are sufficient – your cat shouldn't become replete too soon, but should enjoy the nice taste and want more. A further advantage of small titbits is that the cat won't have to chew too long and instead is ready for the next step of the training sooner.

If you train regularly with your cat, you should deduct the amount of food used during clicker training from her daily feed ration in order to ensure that your cat does not gain excessive weight. If your cat has health problems or if she needs to keep to a specific diet, please ask your vet which titbits are suitable.

Some cats are very difficult to entice with any type of food as a treat. A few suggestions are listed opposite:

- Dry food: the pieces need to be as small as possible; they may need to be broken into bits. Food specifically manufactured for kittens may also be suitable
- Sticks of cat treats (cut up into many small crumbs)
- Different types of cat titbits
- Raw or cooked meat cut into small pieces (try out different types of meat, except pork)
- Malt or vitamin paste
- Portions of yoghurt/cream/sour cream to lick from a spoon
- Your cat's favourite tinned meat to lick from a spoon
- Cheese cubes (try out a variety of types)
- Cream cheese
- A small sip of home-cooked chicken broth

The more delicious the titbits are, the more motivated your cat will be to learn tricks – it is worth the trouble to find out the favourite titbit in a test. (Photo: Nissen)

The selection of possible titbits is very large. Anything is allowed if your cat likes it and it isn't dangerous for her (for example, damaging or poisonous). And of course the main idea is: the healthier the better!

If you and your cat decide that fresh or cooked meat is the right thing for both of you, you can cut the meat into portions for every training session and freeze each portion separately. Simply defrost it for the next day and cut it into cubes shortly before starting the session.

Step Two:
The click sound means 'Correct behaviour!'

Your cat has learned that the click sound always heralds something tasty. It will therefore be delighted if the click is sounded as often as possible. As soon as your cat realises that she can influence you using the clicker and receive a treat with the way she behaves, she will try to repeat this action precisely. If you click as soon as she places her paw onto a small blanket, and immediately give her a reward, your cat will realise that it is worth repeating the action 'Place paw on blanket'. It doesn't matter if your cat performs the trick or the first step towards a trick by pure chance. The click and subsequent reward tells her: 'You have done this correctly; therefore you will now get a reward.' It usually takes a few repetitions until the cat understands precisely how she has managed to make you use the clicker – and from then on she will try to get the click and reward (referred to as 'C & R' from now on) through deliberate behaviour.

This learning process is called operative conditioning or instrumental conditioning. Clicker training uses two variations of this type of learning process. If your cat performs an action and you don't react with the expected click, this behaviour is not rewarding for the cat, but instead frustrating. The cat will soon show this behaviour less frequently and possibly not at all. If, on the other hand, she learns that certain behaviour has positive effects in the form of C & R, she will begin to show this behaviour more frequently. Her behaviour is encouraged in a positive manner. It is this effect which we will utilise during clicker training. You should aim to help your cat achieve as many positive moments and experiences of success as possible during the trick training session.

The precise sequence is the deciding factor, not only in the case of classical conditioning but also in that of operative conditioning. The cat can only learn new tricks during clicker training if the click sounds at the precise moment the cat performs the required action; the reward should be given immediately afterwards.

The deciding factor in the learning process is not what something means to a human, but instead how the animal interprets it! If I stroke my cat as a reward, but she isn't in the mood for it, my stroking is – theoretically speaking, within the context of learning theory – a punishment. At that moment I am doing something unpleasant to her, even if I don't mean it to be.

House cats are rarely as lucky as Plato in coming across a mouse and entertaining themselves in typical cat behaviour. Clicker training is no substitute for hunting and playing, but it is a nice way to entertain an under-challenged cat. (Photo: Dbalý)

For Birne, the pillow is a paw target – if he places his right leg on it he will receive the click and a reward. (Photo: Nissen)

It requires a great deal of concentration, good observational powers and fast reactions to click at the precise moment of the performed action. You have at most half a second to act. If the clicker is used at a later moment, the cat will relate it to her subsequent behaviour and you will have a very confused cat on your hands.

Think back to your clicker game with humans. They do not need classical conditioning to understand the click sound as you can explain the meaning of the click to them in words and the success created by using the clicker during a game acting situation is usually a reward in itself for the human game partner. Therefore, you begin immediately with the operative conditioning; your game partner acts, turns his/her head, makes a step, touches an object and you signal and reward the behaviour positively at the exact same moment as the corresponding action of your partner, thereby motivating him/her to repeat the action or keep trying in order to act correctly.

(Photo: Nissen)

Is everything well planned?
Preparing for clicker training

Before starting to train your cat for the first trick, you need to make a number of practical preparations in order to ensure that the training session will be pleasant, exciting and rewarding for your cat.

Knowing what you want – the training goal

It is an elementary rule that you make a clear decision regarding the aim of the training unit before starting the training session. Consider which steps your cat could present you with on the way to achieving this goal. Don't hesitate to write down the goal and any steps you can think of that will lead the way to achieving it. After the training session, check which of those steps your cat actually took and which ones you didn't expect but rewarded with a click. Also, take note of the length of the training session and the number of clicks – if you know how many titbits you had at the beginning of the training session, simply deduct the ones you still have in your hand to arrive at the number. By doing this you create a small clicker diary. It will help you uncover possible difficulties during the training sessions and react to these. In this way you will observe systematically how your cat reacts during trick training,

which talents she displays, what she and what you find difficult to do and what you need to observe during the training with your cat.

Where and when – training place and time

Where do you intend to do the training sessions? Will you have a quiet environment at the chosen time? You need to make absolutely sure that no children or partners will suddenly burst in during a training session. Other cats that live in the house should not be in the same room to begin with (if that presents you with any difficulties have a look at 'Trick training with several cats' from page 88).

Your cat is entitled to your full concentration and a training session without any interruptions. Be prepared to ignore the telephone, should it ring during the trick training session, or put call barring on (or just unplug it). That way, the training session can develop into a kind of meditation session during which you concentrate entirely on your cat and the training.

Learning is something that occurs by means of associations, such as an action with its consequences. In addition, however, other aspects of the situation are connected with it, which we neither wanted nor planned in the first place. This is particularly true of the training environment. Unchanged training conditions help your cat with her learning process. If the training environment changes, on the other hand, your cat will have to learn an additional concept, namely that if she does sitting up (aka begging for a bone), for example, on the wooden hallway floor as well as on the living room carpet, she will still be successfully rewarded with C & R.

You can write down the following in a training diary:

- The trick you want to achieve (goal) as well as the steps towards it.
- How far have you come?
- Which interim steps did your cat offer?
- Length of the training session.
- Number of clicks.
- Difficulties.

Therefore, try to ensure that your cat has the best conditions possible to start her trick training by initially remaining in the same environment during her trainings sessions.

The term generalisation is used if a cat learns that certain behaviour has the same consequences (such as click and reward) in a variation of framework conditions (changing places, different trainers).

More than just accessories – the training tools

Have all utensils which you will need during the course of the training session at hand before you start. Your cat will not understand that you are simply disappearing because the hoop is still in another room. It could even learn to see it as punishment for whichever behavioural action she presented you with: 'Oh, if I do a sit pretty my human runs away.' That would not be nice!

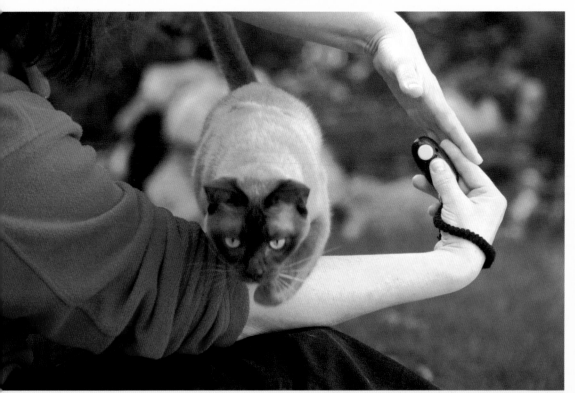

Plato doesn't just jump through the arms of his owner indoors, but out of doors as well. (Photo: Boumala)

You should always make sure that your cat cannot possibly hurt herself on sharp corners, edges, or splinters from any of the objects used. In addition, you should take account of what things your cat prefers and what she doesn't like. A lot of cats don't like to touch plastic. Should your cat feel the same way, choose different materials.

In addition to the objects which you will need for the planned trick, you also need the clicker and the rewards as part of your training implements. Have you already figured out how to manage handing out the titbit rewards during the training session?

One way is to simply hold the reward in your hand. You will be able to offer it to your cat quickly after a click, and you can ensure that your cat won't pinch it. However, in this case you will be restricted in the use of this hand when it comes to using your training tools. In addition, it might occur that rude cats try to get at the food by means of sharpened claws. Until these cats have learned that food doesn't always appear as if by magic, but that they must work for it to be given as a treat, you should select a different receptacle for the food during a training session than your hand. Any type of lockable receptacle, which the human can open easily, but the cat cannot, is suitable. It is worth practising the sequence of 'click, open

container, take out and lay down reward, close container' before the first training session so you will be able to do it quickly during training.

On the other hand, if your cat is more gentle and reserved by nature, or learns the clicking principle very quickly you can try using a small plate to have the titbits to hand. However, you should not ask for too much self-control from your cat by placing the plate right in front of her – after all, your cat needs all her concentration for the trick training. It is fairer to place the rewards plate within easy reach for the trainer but outside the direct view of the cat.

I prefer using feed pouches, used in the training of dogs, which can be fixed to your belt. In order to ensure that the small pieces don't stick to the folds of this pocket, I place a plastic can inside it. This allows you to quickly and easily reach into the bottom of the pouch and you have the feed close at hand without the cat being able to see it.

Short but intensive – the length of a training session

To ensure that trick training is an exciting and fun activity for your cat, she will need a lot of experiences of success. However, this should not be achieved by especially long training sessions, but instead by a large number of clicks and rewards within a short span of time. Any training session can only be successful as long as the cat is still able to concentrate well and as long as the titbit rewards are a real motivational tool. If the cat has had enough to eat, trick training no longer has any meaning and thereby value. If she is unable to concentrate any longer, the danger of making excessive demands and frustrating your cat increases substantially.

In principle, you should always end a training session after your cat has just been very success-ful and earned her C & R, and before she no longer has fun or feels motivated. You can meas-ure the length of a training session by two aspects: the length of time you have been training your cat and the number of C & Rs given. If your feline friend never eats more than a few small portions, you need to limit the training sessions to maybe five or ten clicks. That isn't much, but you don't need to worry – your cat is still able to learn just as much as other cats do. Find out how many tit-bits it takes for your cat to be replete, subtract two titbits and use this number as a general measure. If, on the other hand, your cat is a feline food-processing machine, select a number of titbits (approx. 15 to 20) before you start. Once the tit-bits are gone the training session is over.

As a general rule, you should not just determine the length of the training session by the number of rewards, but also implement a definitive time limit. At the beginning, units of one to a maxi-mum(!) of two minutes are sufficient. The best thing is to have a clock in direct view, because you will be astonished how time flies during clicker training. I rarely work for more than five minutes in one session, even with experienced and very motivated clicker cats. Trick training is an alien task for a cat. She will lose her concen-tration at some point, and the following rule applies to ensure your cat remains motivated: stop the session at the moment when everything is working beautifully.

Did you know that cats hunt at their best when they are not particularly hungry? The inner drive to hunt is independent of the degree of satiety. A starving cat often does not have the required calm and patience to hunt successfully. So, please do not 'starve' your cat in advance of a clicker training session.

As often as you and your cat want

It would be lovely if you did clicker training with your cat regularly and the trick training sessions became a daily ritual. Particularly in the beginning, it helps cats to become used to the training and understand the new principle of clicker training. If you stage short daily training sessions, you will often see first results very quickly, which increases your own fun and motivation. If you cannot (in the long term) continue on a daily basis, it will still work. Your cat is capable of remembering what you did during the last training session even after a few days. She will require a slightly longer preliminary phase of getting used to it, but will subsequently join in the fun with enthusiasm. Cats will remember fully developed tricks that you have taught them for quite a long time. If, on the other hand, you have the necessary time and quiet as well as a highly motivated cat, there is nothing to stop you from doing several short training sessions per day, with lengthy pauses between each session. However, please check very carefully whether your cat is as keen as you are to ensure that you will never overtax her.

The agile Lütti likes to go the full length when he is playing. During trick training he shows that he is intelligent and, with long pauses between each one, several sessions per day are possible. (Photo: Nissen)

(Photo: Boumala)

The time has come:
Introducing trick training

Things become serious in this chapter. You will do your first clicker exercise in a moment, Namely your cat touching the so-called target stick with her nose. Subsequently, you will alternate between carrying out further trick instruc-

tions and additional background knowledge. That way, you will learn to use the clicker as a flexible training tool and how to make successes as easy as possible for your cat.

Touching the target stick with the nose

The goal of the exercise is that the cat touches the end of a stick as soon as she sees it. Once the exercise has been learned, the cat will even cross the room or overcome obstacles in order to be able to touch the target stick.

You can use a variety of things as a target stick, for example pencils, cooking spoons, Chinese chopsticks and other similar objects. The ideal length lies between 20 and a maximum of 60 centimetres.

If your cat is very shy towards humans and is scared of or avoids any touching, you can easily choose an even longer stick. However, you must practise handling this tool without your cat. Subsequently, this exercise with a longer stick will be easier for your cat, as she can keep a greater and safer distance between it and you. If your cat cannot manage to relax reasonably at a distance of less than four feet (1.20 metres) from you, please forgo this exercise and, for example, start with a paw target (see page 63). This allows you to stay at a larger distance.

There are two targets: one, the nose target, where the cat should touch something with her nose, and the other the paw target, where a cat touches an object with her paw. It is within the realm of possibility but clearly so much more difficult to train the cat to touch an object with another part of her body, such as the shoulder or hip.

Faramir follows the target stick and maintains contact with his nose. The slightly hidden position of the trainer makes it easier for a shy cat to carry out this exercise. (Photo: Boumala)

SET-UP

Stage 1

For this exercise we can utilise the natural curiosity of the cat and her tendency to explore new objects with her nose. In order to make success as rapid as possible for your cat we ensure that the first steps are carried out in a very simple manner. Gently move one end of the target stick at an angle from the front to the shoulder of your cat. Stop no later than when the stick is about a hand's width from your cat (you do not actively touch the cat with the stick). The end of the stick should unobtrusively be close enough to the cat so that she can touch it with just a bare minimum of movement of her head. As soon as your cat shows the first impulse of movement in the direction of the stick, use the clicker and lay or hold the stick out of reach for a moment while you give your cat her reward. Once she has eaten the titbit start with round 2. Hold the stick in the same way within reach of your cat. If she touches the stick with the nose, follow with C & R.

Does your cat belong to the rare type that resists the temptation and won't automatically move her nose towards the stick? In this case your skills as a trainer and using precise observational skills are required. It is very rare that a cat manages to completely ignore an object that has been moved in her immediate surroundings. Please use the clicker at the precise moment at which your cat takes her first fleeting glance at the target stick. In this way your cat will soon learn that the stick must have something positive about it and, after a few 'glance clicks', will force herself to actually inspect the stick more closely with her nose – C & R follow.

A playful cat in particular may want to touch and pull at the target stick with her paw. That action will not earn her any C & R. Instead, observe every slightest forward movement that your cat takes with her neck and head in the direction of the target stick without a raised paw, for you to be able to use the clicker as a reward for any advance with her nose towards the stick.

If your cat has touched the target stick with her nose several times and without hesitation, you can congratulate yourself and your cat; she has already understood the first step of the exercise!

Stage 2

At this stage you can up the ante and slightly increase the degree of difficulty. Point the target stick towards your cat again, but this time approximately 3 to 4 centimetres further away than before. Your cat still doesn't have to get up to touch the stick, but she will have to stretch a bit. As soon as she does that, immediately give her C & R. Repeat this a few times until your cat stretches her nose towards the stick reliably; either a bit up or down, a bit to the right side and then to the other.

If you are still in your very first training session with the target stick, end the session for the day. You will probably have given your cat plenty of C & R, and both of you have come a long way!

This stage of the training process can pose the possible danger of overtaxing the cat by moving the stick too far away, too quickly. In that case, the cat will only look at the stick, if that, but won't move towards it. As we want to make this training as easy as possible for her, it suffices for the cat to take just one step towards the target stick, so she can reach out and touch it.

Possible steps towards the goal

- Looking towards the target stick (TS)
- Nose touches TS from a short distance
- Stretching the neck to touch the TS
- Getting up in order to reach the TS with the nose
- Taking a step and touching the TS
- Taking several steps towards the TS

Stage 4
If your cat has been willing to take this one step several times, move the stick back by the length of a thumb at your next attempt and ask your cat for a second step – which will, of course, be followed immediately with C & R. In this way you can slowly increase the distance between your cat and the target stick by means of many small steps and a number of training units and thus make the action ever harder to follow. It doesn't mean,

Getting started is easy: the target stick is held in such a way that Faramir has to lift his head slightly to touch the stick with his nose. (Photo: Boumala)

Stage 3
For some cats the next step is a very big one: now she needs to get up in order to touch the target stick and thus earn her C & R. Even if your cat already stands during this training unit, simply stretching out for the stick won't be enough any longer. Instead she is going to have to move more than previously.

however, that you go ahead directly – it can be frustrating if everything simply becomes more and more difficult to carry out. Surprise your cat at intervals by offering the stick at a close distance and allow her to earn C & R with no more than a 'relaxed movement of her head'.

Did your cat take a step towards the target several times during the last training session? In your next session go back a step and reinforce the memory of your cat regarding this exercise, by moving the target stick so close that she only needs to move her nose slightly. Depending on how fast your cat performs the actions you ask her to do, both of you can progress forward jointly either with a few or a lot of repetitions of the individual steps, right up to the point of what your cat learned at the end of your prior training session. It is perfectly OK, and often well timed, to simply strengthen the fundamental instructions for the actions your cat has learned so far, by repeating those training steps, before moving on with the training.

You can introduce diversity into the game, by not using the target stick exclusively on the ground. Before the start of the training session place a chair at an accessible distance to your cat. Instead of asking your cat to take a dozen steps towards the target stick, show her the stick on or above the chair. Now your cat will have to jump on the chair in order to be able to touch the target with her nose.

Variations

Instead of moving towards the target stick, the cat can also be taught to follow it with her nose. During this exercise, the cat will need to increase the time she maintains nose contact with the stick to earn her C & R. In order to teach this to the cat, you need to delay the click by a second when your cat is moving her nose into the correct position. If she keeps her nose on the stick, follow with C & R. Repeat this exercise several times. After that, increase the length of time your cat needs to keep nose contact with the target. Don't move forward too quickly with this exercise, and shorten the length of time you expect the cat to maintain contact at regular intervals.

The next challenge is for the cat to keep nose contact with the target stick in movement. In other words, she needs to learn to connect the nose touching exercise with movement – which is not at all easy. Therefore, at the start of teaching this exercise, please reduce the length of time your cat remains in contact with the stick, and as before introduce the new exercise in small steps.

If you are training ten cats to do the same trick, you will realise that you are observing ten different processes. The basic principle remains the same but the cats differ in what they have to offer, at what speed they offer it, how fast they think of a new step, how long they wish to train during each training unit, and so forth. A good trainer will always take these differences into account and support each cat individually with regard to their talents and potential.

Never use the target stick to lead your cat into a situation which is uncomfortable for her or frightens her. A cat that follows the target stick may be so concentrated on doing the exercise that she isn't consciously aware of her environment. That can produce a really huge shock for your cat after C & R, once she becomes aware of her environment again. Trick training should be a fun thing and help your cat gain self-confidence – impulses which trigger fear are definitely not part of the programme.

Finger target

The cat touches your pointing finger with her nose. She moves towards this outstretched finger when she sees it or follows it when the finger moves.

SET-UP

Variation 1
Teaching the finger target is set up in the same way as touching the target stick. Click and reward the cat's reaching out to the finger: looking, stretching the neck, getting up, taking a step forward towards the finger. At the same time, start with the easiest step, by taking your pointed

Faramir is learning to touch the finger instead of the target stick. For this purpose the target stick is clandestinely removed. (Photo: Boumala)

finger within view of the cat she only has to turn her head very slightly in order to touch it with her nose.

If your cat has an issue with body contact and moves back when you bring your hand so close to her head, you should never perform this exercise when the trick training is still new for your cat. Just keep on working with the target stick exercise and create more positive experiences for your cat with the tricks where she won't have to overcome her fears immediately.

Variation 2

The prerequisite for the second variation of teaching your cat the finger target is complete mastery of the target stick exercise. Once your cat touches the target stick reliably with her nose, takes a number of steps towards it and touches it, or willingly follows it, you can 'clandestinely remove' the target stick. Instead of holding the stick right at your end, move your hand forward bit by bit towards the end that your cat touches. At the same time place the finger against the target stick in such a way that it points to the tip of the target stick. At some stage, the tip of your finger will replace the end of the target stick. Do not expect your cat to immediately perform the exercise with the finger target with the same degree of proficiency as she does it with the target stick. Lead her slowly through the different degrees of difficulty and build up the exercise with care.

(Photo: Nissen)

The first technique towards the completed trick:
Shaping

Do you have any idea what you have accomplished during the training with the target stick as well as with the finger target, and also during the clicker game with other people? You have successfully made yourself acquainted with the first technique of teaching a trick by making use of the clicker: shaping.

Shaping up the trick

Shaping literally means the process of forming the behaviour of the cat. We have a goal in our head and slowly and gently shape the behaviour of the cat in the correct direction until she carries out the target behaviour we envisaged. The cat determines how many steps are needed to reach the goal. The process of shaping requires us to observe our cat very closely, so that we notice even her smallest but very important movements. In the beginning that can be hard work, because it is not exactly something you do regularly. However, you won't just be rewarded by the advances in the training process of your cat but also by the fact that you will get to know your cat on a far deeper level!

ZsiZsa waves with her left paw. The trainer can use shaping to bring the height of the paw into the desired position. (Photo: Nissen)

If you find it difficult to recognise the small movements your cat makes during the training sessions and to strengthen them with C & R, play the clicker game with another person as often as you can to develop more routine in your training sessions. You can also closely observe your cat during a normal day, for example when she is playing or eating, but also when you are cuddling her gently, to help you get more experience. Which tiny little movements does your cat make? Does she move the end of her tail? Does she turn her head very slightly? Does she extend her whiskers? Does she tense her body?

Shaping a trick has many advantages:

1. The cat is required to think. She needs to find which of her actions have the effect on us to respond with C & R. This will encourage her creativity, she tries out new things all the time – and

gains many successes. This is a marvellous experience especially for shy, timid, and passive cats.

2. The cat determines the tempo and is able to decide on her own how far she wants to proceed. This is an important factor for exercises which require her to overcome her reservations. She will never be pushed to do something but instead is rewarded with C & R in her courageous approach for every tiny step in the right direction – because even a tiny little step can require a lot of courage!

3. Clicker training uses absolutely no physical force – not even a gentle one. Never push, pick up, set down, shove, knock down or outstare your cat. She is allowed to act solely of her own free will.

For your first tricks you should select training tools which you can put away after the training session. Otherwise your cat could continue the exercise and become frustrated because she no longer receives C & R. She could, for example, jump on a chair just after you have been teaching her this very thing. Experienced clicker cats learn that certain types of behaviour and tricks are only rewarded in the context of a training session, or if you have given her a signal. However, it will take some time before you have reached this stage!

Sit on the blanket

This exercise teaches the cat to sit on a blanket and wait there in a relaxed manner, until she receives a different signal.

For this exercise you should select a blanket made from a material that your cat likes, for example a towel, a place mat, a large coaster made from cork or a folded fleece blanket. In order not to confuse your cat, please don't take a blanket that is always available for your cat, but select a new one which will only be used for this trick. Choose a size which allows your cat to sit comfortably on the blanket.

SET-UP

Stage 1
Take your clicker, titbits, the blanket and your cat to the training area. Have your hand on the clicker, allowing you to use it while you are still standing. Observe your cat while you are placing the blanket on the floor. The chance of your cat looking curiously at it at that precise moment is very high – this is the right moment for the first click, followed immediately, as always, by a reward. Unlike the target stick, leave the blanket on the floor undisturbed, whilst your cat eats her titbit.

If your cat is still some distance away from the blanket you will probably feel like giving her the reward closer to the blanket. After all, your cat is supposed to move in the direction of the blanket. Please resist this impulse. Instead place the reward on the floor right next to your cat. This way, you will make it very easy for your cat to earn her next click as quickly as possible, simply by turning her head back towards the blanket.

Often, the trainer misses the first opportunity to click during a trick training exercise, namely the moment when you place the training object on the floor and your cat takes a first look at it. It is very easy to miss this moment because the trainer isn't concentrating on the trick training session yet. If you aim to be a good and attentive trainer, you need to test and practise the handling of all objects before you start teaching your cat to learn the trick. The very first glance by your cat towards the object is the perfect moment to tell her, 'Exactly, this is today's goal!'

The speed at which a cat will move towards a new blanket differs. Some cats like to ignore a new object for a while, before starting to explore it. It may be that they check passively whether that curious thing really IS harmless. In that case you need to be extremely observant, register even the slightest glance and the smallest hint of movement in the right direction and use the clicker to mark these improvements. Is your cat really ignoring the blanket completely? In that case,

Shaping on the blanket: approach, then three paws and finally Faramir sits on the blanket in textbook perfection. (Photos: Boumala)

move the blanket on the floor very gently for a moment, keeping your eyes on your cat, of course. The movement will arouse her curiosity; she looks at it for a moment – C & R! After a few repetitions, your cat will begin to get interested in the blanket. However, that may not happen until the second or third training session.

Other cats, their curiosity aroused, will walk up to the blanket immediately. If your cat does that, immediately click and reward her. Place the reward at a very slight angle away from the direction your cat moved. Next use the clicker if your cat turns towards the blanket again. When she takes a further step towards the blanket – C & R. Resist the temptation to hold back the next click and watch whether your bold cat, which walked right up to the blanket in the first place, might possibly sit on it directly. And the reason for this? What will you do if your cat suddenly changes direction close to the blanket and walks away from it? That would mean a huge missed opportunity for lots of clicking and rewarding your cat.

The very first tricks that a cat learns during clicker training imprint particularly well, and your cat will perform them happily. With that in mind, the trainer should choose them with care. The latest research has also shown that things a cat learns through clicker training are generally particularly well embedded in the cat's memory.

Therefore, especially at the beginning of an exercise, keep your steps as short as possible, and instead click and reward your cat more frequently. The higher the frequency of rewards, the more enjoyment your cat will have in performing this trick and the easier she will be able to learn.

Stage 2

If your cat moves towards the blanket and already understands that there is something going on with this thing, you can start the next training phase: stepping onto the blanket. Maybe your cat sniffs at the blanket first? That means immediate C & R. If your cat sniffs it again, use the clicker again. To begin with, she needs a lot of affirmations. After a few repetitions, don't react with the clicker any more but wait instead. Your cat now needs to think of something else to earn a click. Does she touch the blanket carefully with her paw? In that case she gets C & R. Does she lift her paw above the blanket? C & R. Does she place a paw onto the blanket? C & R.

Reward everything that the cat offers a few times. After that, stop using the clicker for this action and let your cat try out which next step in the session will earn her the next click. At some point it is no longer sufficient for the cat to place a paw on the blanket – the second paw needs to follow. If you give your cat her reward directly on the blanket, if she has placed both front paws onto the blanket, the following step will be very difficult to understand and she may not know what she is supposed to do. Therefore, place the titbit right next to the blanket. In that way, your cat can then repeat placing both paws back onto the blanket and successfully earn her reward. If that doesn't work, lower the requirements and give your cat C & R after she places just one paw onto the blanket again.

Stage 3

After placing both front paws on the blanket, cats usually don't offer the third paw and get onto the blanket with all four paws instead. Do however click at the moment the third paw touches the blanket. Otherwise, it could happen that the cat walks onto and over the blanket - and you certainly don't want to use the clicker at the moment the cat leaves the blanket! Rewards are placed next to the blanket again and you click again when the cat steps onto the blanket. Repeat this training stage until the cat will step onto the blanket time and time again.

Stage 4

If, at any time, your cat sits down on the blanket without being told, use the clicker and reward her for this action. If on the other hand, she always stands reliably on the blanket, don't use the clicker and instead wait. Your cat will now have to offer something new. She will probably look at you expectantly – and may sit down while she waits for you to click and reward her at last. You will do that as soon as the cat shows any movement that leads to sitting down. Still place the rewards next to the blanket. The current status is as follows: stepping onto the blanket and sitting down leads to C & R.

Do not forget to consolidate this stage, by repeating it several times!

Possible steps on the way to the goal:

- Looking towards the blanket
- Signs of moving in the direction of the blanket
- Moving towards the blanket
- Tentative sniffing at the blanket
- First paw on the blanket
- Two paws on the blanket
- Four paws on the blanket
- Sitting down on the blanket
- Staying put on the blanket

Stage 5

The last step towards a successful trick means teaching your cat to remain seated on the blanket for longer and earning C & R that way. Before you begin with this step, please think about how much staying power you can ask of your cat. Is your cat young or particularly active? In this case, expecting your cat to sit on the blanket for 10 seconds is an incredible achievement. Therefore, please don't overtax your cat through excessively high expectations, and be patient.

The new criterion is the time your cat stays sitting on the blanket. Again, increase the time by the same small amounts as you did with the advance towards the blanket. Don't click your cat at the exact moment she sits down, but instead a second later when she is already sitting down. Attention: now give her the reward on the blanket. Wait a second or two. Is your cat still sitting on the blanket? C & R on the blanket. Wait another second or two to see if she remains seated! Another C & R. In this manner your cat learns that she can earn a titbit if she remains sitting patiently on the blanket. Perfect! Now wait four seconds. If your cat remains seated calmly, click and give her the reward next to the blanket, so she leaves the blanket to get at the reward. This way, your cat does not leave the blanket because she has lost interest, but instead because you have encouraged her to do so.

If your cat does not wait but leaves the blanket, don't stop her in any way and don't react to her behaviour either. This isn't a negative thing – after all, your cat is still learning. Use the next opportunity for C & R, when your cat walks onto the blanket again, when she sits down, and when she remains on the blanket.

Increase the time span your cat remains seated on the blanket very slowly in many training sessions, and don't forget to make it surprisingly easy for your cat from time to time. That increases the enjoyment factor for your cat.

Variations

Teach your cat to sit on the blanket in different surroundings/locations. This is a new learning achievement which is quite difficult, as the cat has to generalise. To begin with, you can simply move the blanket a few centimetres every time, while your cat gets her reward placed next to the blanket. Increase the distance moved slowly! For example, sometimes place the blanket on the carpet and sometimes on the wooden floor. Increase your distance from your cat. Wander around the entire room. After this, take your cat and the blanket into the next room.

The goal of this exercise is not for the cat to sit motionless on her little blanket for hours. If you teach this trick well, your cat can wait on the blanket for a few minutes. In that case you need to reward her often, because this exercise may require a great deal of self-control. As compensation you may play with her for a while or follow up with a trick that requires more activity.

Place a thin cushion underneath the blanket, which changes its height. No problem? In that case place the blanket on a sturdy low box, on a thick book or on a suitcase. If all these variations work like clockwork, increase the height of these bases until only the edge of the blanket is visible to the cat, and she needs to jump on top of it. Ensure that your construction is slide-proof and can't topple over.

You can construct all other tricks that require your cat to stand on an object with all four or maybe only with the two front paws of using this same principle.

'Here's looking at you, kid!' With the help of shaping, Faramir has learned to keep eye contact for longer. This exercise has fabulous effects when handling cats, which as a rule are a bit shy towards humans and tend to regard direct eye contact as threatening. (Photo: Boumala)

During normal training sessions it is the best method to use titbits as a reward. However, during the normal daily routine, you can surprise your cat with creative rewards and improve your communication with her.

Your cat wants you to let her out onto the balcony? Ask her to perform a trick you have already taught her, use the clicker and open the door as a reward.

The most important rules of shaping according to Karen Pryor

Karen Pryor formulated the famous 'Laws of Shaping' a long time ago. These are set out here in sections and in a slightly changed form to apply to trick training with cats:

• Increase the requirements in steps that are small enough for your cat to have a realistic chance of being successful and to reach consolidation.

• Always practise just one detail of behaviour, never two at the same time.

• During the introduction of a new detail regarding the trick, permit your cat to temporarily perform less well than she has previously.

• Always be a step ahead of your cat. Plan the individual training steps carefully in advance, so that you know what you want to demand next from your cat, even if your cat suddenly surprises you with a higher level of improvement.

• Your cat can easily do trick training with different people. However, only one trainer should commence a new trick, because the differently applied criteria for C & R could otherwise confuse your cat. Once she has internalised the trick, other people can also ask her to perform it.

• If an exercise is unsuccessful, look for another way. Many roads lead to Rome – maybe a different one is more pleasant or easier to understand for your cat.

• Don't interrupt a training session without a reason – your cat may see this as a punishment, even if you didn't mean it that way at all.

• If your cat performs the trick badly, go back a few steps and shape it again until the cat shows the behaviour you aimed for. In that way you help your cat to remember what she has been taught and to understand the point of the trick.

• End every trick training session with a rewarding experience for your cat. You should also end the training session while you are still ahead by a step.

(Photo: Nissen)

The second technique towards the completed trick:
Support with targets or titbits

To work out a trick through shaping is fabulous, amongst other things because the cat needs to think and try out different actions. Of course we can utilise the natural explorative behaviour of our cats for the shaping process. In the case of certain tricks, however, shaping can also be very exhausting and even confusing for the cat. In this case, targets or titbits offer better support.

Sit pretty (aka: Begging for a bone)

For this trick we need a type of behaviour which, from the point of view of the cat, isn't something she would do outside the training process and without a definite incentive. Balancing on her hind legs without any support from the front paws is shown by a cat in two situations: she will do this either to investigate an area she cannot see clearly, or to reach up to an object at greater height with the front paws.

If you were to try to shape this trick, you would start with your cat sitting down. Every upward tilt of the head, every lifting of the shoulders and neck is rewarded with a click and reward. It sounds arduous, as well as difficult for the cat to understand – and it certainly is.

Therefore, in order to teach the cat to do sitting up with great fun and without any frustration, we deviate from the clicker principle not to entice the cat at individual moments.

SET-UP

Keep your clicker ready and take a titbit in your hand where the cat can see it. Hold this titbit between your thumb and middle finger while pointing your index finger upwards. You may be familiar with this gesture as a signal for a dog to sit – I like to use it as a 'sit pretty' signal. Now lift the hand that is holding the titbits in front of your cat until it hovers one or two hand's-widths above your cat's head. Does your cat follow this movement with her eyes? If so, she gets immediate C & R – however, you must give her her titbit with the other hand! When your cat has finished eating, repeat the process. Lift the hand with the titbit in front of your cat. If you observe

any attempt at moving upwards, stretching the head, lifting one paw from the floor, stretching one paw upward, doing a sit pretty, click and reward each step.

Only encourage your cat to show attempts for a certain body posture or a certain action with titbits if you know that your cat is gentle towards you. If she shows any inclination to grab her feed with an outstretched paw, dismiss this idea for now. You should not get injured during trick training and your cat should not be allowed to earn titbits through brute force. Instead, choose variation 1 with the target stick or the finger target.

As a rule, the titbit in your hand encourages your cat to offer you a range of behaviours, which enables you to click on the way to the goal. In that way, she gets to earn a lot of clicks and decides that the exercise is good fun. She learns that your hand above her head offers the opportunity for C & R. After a few repeats you can start using just your hand with the finger pointed as usual – without a titbit in that hand. Your cat will still continue to offer actions in the direction of the hand, which enables you to shape her into performing the correct sit pretty.

When you train your cat using the same hand positioning all the time, it has a nice side-effect: your cat automatically learns a hand signal for this trick.

Variation 1

If your cat is already familiar with the target stick or the finger target, you can also use these to show your cat the sit pretty position. For that purpose, don't hold the target stick at the normal height of the cat, but instead hold it close to your cat yet a bit higher, and click if she stretches upwards towards the stick. Increase this in small steps until your cat holds up both paws and sits down on her hind legs in order to touch the stick. If your cat reaches for the target stick dangling over her head with one paw, she shows typical cat behaviour. Simply ignore it and instead reward her with a click after her next attempt of an upward movement of her head or body.

Only encourage your cat to learn variations of an exercise if the cat has already mastered the basic trick safely for some time. Otherwise, there is a real danger that the similarity of the trick variations confuses the cat and leads to frustration.

Variation 2

A difficult variation of the sit-up trick is for the cat no longer to sit on her haunches but to stand on them instead. It requires more strength and in

Lütti demonstrates a perfectly balanced sit pretty standing on her hind legs (Variation 2). (Photo: Nissen)

particular a great deal of balance and body consciousness.

You can shape such a tall standing cat if you observe your cat very precisely. The next time she does a sit pretty don't use the clicker. Your cat will be slightly irritated, as she usually gets a titbit for that movement and she has performed it well. She will probably do another sit pretty and intensify the movement slightly. As soon as the cat shows a slightly higher posture when doing this, C & R. Take care to keep your demands to a minimum level at first, with plenty of opportunities of successes for your cat – otherwise she may no longer find sitting pretty a fun thing to do.

As an alternative, you can also encourage your cat to stand on her hind legs with just a few repeated tries with a titbit or the target stick. Make your cat sit up on her haunches. Then move the titbit up a bit over the cat's head. Your cat will stretch up to get closer to the titbit – that means immediate C & R with a titbit from your other hand. If you slightly alter the position of your hand for this repeated entice, for example by holding the titbit between the thumb, the middle and the ring finger, and point up your index and small finger, your cat learns a second signal. This defines sitting pretty and standing on her hind legs as two different exercises.

Jumping over an obstacle

Your cat jumps over an obstacle. For this purpose, build a small jump or fix a small plank of wood in such a way that your cat can jump over it. The obstacle should be about as high as the shoulder or back of your cat. That way, it is a bit too high for the cat simply to walk across it. At

Birne even performs sitting pretty on the back of his trainer. In his eagerness he stretches a bit too far towards the signalling hand – not visible in the photo. (Photo: Nissen)

the same time, however, your cat can see what's on the other side of the jump. To begin with, the obstacle should be at least 50 to 60 centimetres wide, otherwise the temptation of simply running around may be too great. It also helps if you create a wing on at least one side by placing the jump at a ninety-degree angle against a piece of furniture or a wall. In addition, the jump should reach down to the floor, to stop your cat from crawling underneath it.

The important thing is that the obstacle must be stable and sturdy, even if the cat steps on it. You need to ensure that there is no danger of injury to the cat, and that she won't be startled if the jump collapses with a great deal of noise.

Faramir learns to jump over a new jump with the help of the target stick. (Photo: Boumala)

A nice alternative to jumping over an obstacle is for your cat to jump across your stretched out or folded legs. If you push your feet against a chest of drawers or a sofa, you can keep this position without having to flex your muscles too much, and you can also slightly alter the height of the leg jump.

SET-UP

Of course, jumping over an obstacle can be shaped. Possible interim steps for C & R would be: the cat looks towards the obstacle, moves towards the obstacle, touches it with her nose, looks over the jump to the other side, touches it with her paw, stretches upwards to have a better look over the other side, leans forward, places one paw on top of the obstacle, two paws on top of the obstacle, jumps.

On the other hand, there is no reason why you should not make the start of the very first obstacle jump easier for your cat, by literally helping her to get over the first hurdle: you can use either the finger target or the target stick and also entice your cat with food. I will describe the set-up of the exercise with the aid of an enticement.

Sit down on one side of the obstacle. Take a titbit in your hand, show it to your cat and move it along the running track and jump-off, and over the jump in front of your cat. Point your finger as you would for the finger target. In addition, you

Jumping over the trainer's legs can be set up in the same manner as jumping over obstacles. To begin with, Eazy hesitates and receives a click and a reward for showing a first approach by placing his paws on the trainer's leg. Then he overcomes his doubts and eventually even accomplishes the jump over the leg through the hoop. (Photos: Nissen)

should tap your finger on the floor behind the obstacle approximately where your cat will land. Did your cat follow your finger and titbit over the obstacle? Click at the exact moment that your cat leaps over the jump and give her her reward. Repeat this process and lead your cat over the other side of the jump in the same position with your hand holding the titbit and tapping the floor as before. Once this works quite reliably, repeat the enticement another two or three times. Don't give the cat the titbit that you are using as an enticement, but instead the 'reward' one in the other hand. Later perform only the movement of the hand without holding a titbit. Your cat will learn very quickly that it is worth jumping over the obstacle by just following the hand signal.

The signal described for the jump over the obstacle consists of an optical and an acoustic component. The cat sees your finger pointing over/behind the obstacle and hears the tapping sound behind it. If you practise this exercise often enough, your cat will understand the two signals, even if you only use one at a time. If she hears the tapping behind any obstacle, she knows that this is an opportunity to earn herself C & R by jumping over it.

If you give your cat a bit of support by using a target or by enticing her, you can and should use this immediately to create a hand signal for this trick. In the case of all other training techniques, using the clicker means the signal will come at the end, namely when the cat has understood the exercise one hundred percent. Therefore, you don't have to start worrying about hand signals during the performance of all the tricks you are teaching your cat. We will deal with that later.

(Photo: Nissen)

The third technique towards the completed trick:
Capturing

In addition to the traditional techniques of trick training, shaping and 'cheating' with target stick or enticing, there is another option to teach a cat a trick – so-called capturing. It means that you can capture behavioural actions of your cat which you would like to add to your repertoire of tricks with the clicker, if your cat displays them spontaneously – within a training session, but mainly if your cat shows certain behaviour during the normal daily routine.

Capturing spontaneous behaviour – always ready

Capturing is particularly useful for the kind of tricks which would be very difficult and protracted to shape, as well as for all natural mannerisms and movements that the cat displays as part of her playful or comfort actions.

Capturing requires that you are permanently ready – namely ready to click. Just as during a 'normal' training unit, the deciding factor during capturing is that you click at the right moment, and that is precisely the instant at which the cat displays the action you want her to do. If your cat has already ended that particular action, it is too late for the click! It isn't quite as dramatic if you take a second longer to present the reward. However, a reward must follow under all circumstances and as quickly as possible. Get used to carrying a clicker and a little tin of titbits around in your trouser pocket at all times (if you use your tongue to click, you have a clear advantage for capturing).

You can also place several clickers and titbit tins in different areas of the home, to have them permanently available. Once you are prepared for it, you can then capture an entire range of tricks wonderfully. You need to teach your cat a signal for that particular behaviour in order to turn the cat's spontaneous behaviour into a trick you can then ask for at any time.

'Where are you, Eazy?' 'Miaow'. For cats that are allowed outside, a miaow in answer to a signal could be a life-saving exercise that you can teach your cat through capturing. (Photo: Nissen)

Signals

When we use the clicker, we give neither commands nor orders. Instead, we give our cat signals which tell her: 'You now have an opportunity to earn C & R by displaying certain behaviour.'

Introducing a signal requires that the cat already knows the trick and carries out the behaviour related to it smoothly. That is the case after a successful shaping and after a number of repetitions. This may mean differences, depending on the cat and the trick. As before, we normally wait with the introduction of a signal, until the cat has obviously understood the exercise. If you frequently capture a desired behaviour with the clicker, your cat will soon display this behaviour in your presence more often. Once the opportunities for C & R become more and more frequent, and your cat has obviously understood that her behaviour is a trick, it is time to introduce a signal.

At this stage, you need to observe your cat as closely as possible: what makes you recognise that your cat is on the brink of carrying out the behaviour you want to capture in a moment's time? Display the signal a split second before she performs the definitive movement. Then use your clicker while the cat is performing that behaviour and subsequently reward her.

The timeline is as follows: signal – behaviour and click at the same time – reward. There should be less than a second between all the individual components, and that is not an easy thing for us humans.

From now on, the desired behaviour will only be rewarded with success, in other words through C & R, if you gave the signal in advance. It will

be very frustrating for your cat, if a certain behaviour suddenly stops working, in other words does not earn a click or reward. Therefore, give her as many opportunities as possible to earn her C & R by displaying the trick behaviour, after you have given her the signal. As a rule, it will take many repetitions to ensure that your cat fully understands and has internalised the connection between the signal and her behaviour.

What is a good signal?

Cats tend to react better to non-verbal body language signals than to words. This is probably because we as humans tend to talk for 12 hours per day and it isn't easy for the cat to filter out the relevant moments of trick training. However, even amongst themselves, cats have the tendency to 'talk' with each other more through body language than verbally. Therefore, I prefer to work with body language signals, in particular with hand signals. However, these can be coupled with the verbal signals if they are displayed at the same time right from the beginning.

Irrespective of whether you use verbal or non-verbal signals, it is important that you are able to repeat them at any time and in the exact same way. You must make sure not to use them during the day without the possibility of C & R, as it will otherwise confuse your cat. Therefore, it is very practical to use words in a different language if you use verbal signals.

Why won't it work?

If a cat doesn't react to a signal she doesn't do that for the sake of annoying you. She is neither obstinate nor stubborn. The three most common reasons why a cat does not react to a signal are as follows:

1. Your cat hasn't made the connection between the signal and the action – in other words, so far she doesn't understand it at all. The reason for that could be because you haven't repeated it often enough, but also could also arise from bad timing regarding the introduction of the signal. Like a trick itself, the signal needs to be generalised, in other words the cat needs to learn that it is valid in different environments.

2. The cat is momentarily distracted or is unable to concentrate, because of disturbance outside the training area, the other cat/cats (if you have more than one) threatening her in a subtle manner by staring at her, the phone ringing, or she is too hungry. There are more important – vital – matters than a trick signal. Therefore, ensure you create a calm and relaxed training environment, and then have another go at teaching the signal.

3. Your cat is not sufficiently motivated. Is she awake and healthy and not already exhausted from any other activities? Are the rewards really adequate for the performance which your cat offers? Only your cat can answer this question. Why don't you ask her by offering a more attractive reward?

Rolling

The cat lies down and rolls from one side to the other once.

SET-UP

It is possible but quite difficult to shape the trick of rolling on her back from side to side. A prerequisite is that, within the overall training, the cat is already lying on the floor and is still moving about in that position. However, the most likely movement that your cat will offer within the training session is to get up, which you aren't really allowed to click and reward. Therefore, I would recommend that only very experienced trainers should shape the roll. It should be possible to lead a cat, which has to be lying down, into the rolling movement, by enticing her with a titbit, which you need to pass over the cat's shoulder, and use the clicker during this movement. This description of teaching the rolling trick is quite common, the application/execution on the other hand is quite difficult, and the risk that the cat will use her front paws to catch the hand with the titbit (successfully and probably at least slightly painfully) is great.

Stage 1

You will find that it is much easier, faster, and more transparent to capture the rolling in the form of a trick. Observe your cat attentively during the day. There are a number of different typical situations in which a cat rolls on the floor, either as a precursor to play or during a playing session itself, as an invitation to stroke her, during rubbing and wriggling on her back, or simply enjoying a pleasant or exciting smell. Utilise the

Plato rolls on his back from the left side to the right to get the click and reward. In his mind, rolling from the right side to the left is a different trick. (Photos: Boumala)

moment and click when the cat carries out the rolling movement from one side to the other. Your cat will probably be fairly astonished that it gets C & R outside a training session. However, it will soon realise that this happens more frequently while it is rolling around on the floor. And as a result you will soon find that your cat starts to roll around the floor more frequently when you are around – which you will respond to with C & R as often as possible.

Stage 2

If you are sure that your cat already offers the rolling movement on purpose, you can start introducing a signal. You will need a good talent for observation in order to recognise the sign just before your cat is about to roll on her back from side to side (lifting of the upper front leg, a slight turn of the head, but also a 'crazy' look while she asks you to play with her). Immediately before she rolls, perform the signal. Use the clicker for the rolling motion and then reward your cat immediately. Repeat the action a few times: signal for rolling, rolling and click, reward. Then eliminate the signal if you see the attempt for rolling, and just let your cat roll. This time don't use the clicker for that – from now on your cat can only earn herself C & R if you showed her the corresponding signal beforehand.

This represents a huge learning curve for your cat, because if you don't click following the rolling, your cat will be surprised and frustrated. As she needs to experience further successes under all circumstances, please continue to use the so-called 'spontaneous offers of rolling' of your cat, always link these with the signal, and give your cat plenty of opportunities to earn C & R by rolling after you show her the signal to roll. In the course of this, stop using the signal, and thereby also C & R, every now and then. This

Hand signals for rolling

There are no hard and fast rules regarding the choice of which specific signal you use for whatever trick or exercise you are training. Your cat won't understand any hand signal automatically. Instead each signal only gains its meaning if we introduce it reliably and at the right time, thereby allowing the cat to link it with a certain behaviour that is worth carrying out (C & R).

Therefore, I won't recommend a fixed hand signal for rolling – you can make up your own. Of course, you need to make sure that your cat can tell the difference between it and other hand signals. And once you have used it for the first time during training, you should not change it – not even by slight nuances – otherwise you will make things unnecessarily difficult for your cat.

Faramir reacts to the signal of a closed fist by licking his right paw. (Photo: Boumala)

allows your cat to slowly learn that there is a specific signal for rolling, which announces a possibility of a reward. That way she retains the fun element of performing this exercise.

Over time, transfer the signal into the normal trick training process. Show your cat the signal for rolling – and wait a little. Your cat now has to perform an incredible transfer performance, and that could take some time. If she has understood the signal, she will now roll over on her back. If she doesn't perform an entire rollover but makes an attempt, please use the clicker and reward her for her performance! At this stage, your cat will have a fairly good idea what you are expecting from her but isn't quite sure yet if she is right. You can then 'shape up' the rolling process within the course of a training session, and continue to connect the spontaneously offered rolling process with the signal and then use the clicker.

Grooming

The cat licks her outstretched paw once with her tongue.

SET-UP

Observe your cat when she grooms herself and wait for the moment when she lifts up one front leg and licks it with her tongue (as a rule, she does that in order to wash herself over the head with that leg). At the exact moment of the first lick you need to follow up with C & R. Repeat this process regularly, whenever your cat performs this movement during her grooming time.

After a while your cat will offer you this grooming movement more frequently. At this stage, you can introduce a signal for grooming, by showing it to your cat immediately before she proceeds to lick her leg. Over time, after having carried out the process a number of times, show your cat the signal within the framework of a normal clicker training session, when she isn't actually grooming herself. If your cat has already connected the signal with her action, she will offer you a lovely grooming trick. If your cat still has problems performing it, she hasn't understood the connection between signal and action and will require more repetitions during her normal grooming time.

Attention: if your cat licks her coat excessively, tears out her fur, or frequently displays a short grooming session under extreme stress in the form of a displacement activity, please eliminate this trick from your repertoire. Frequent and hectic grooming or exaggerated long grooming sessions, during which the cat develops bald patches, need to be taken seriously as an indication of a number of ailments and/or high stress levels – in that case you need to act immediately.

101 things to do with ...!

This is one of the few exercises where you as the trainer aren't following a definitively planned goal. Quite the opposite, in fact; you want your cat to achieve as many different things as possible with each respective training tool. The actual goal is on a higher level; the exercise encourages your cat to be creative.

The classical tool for introducing this exercise is a cardboard box. For example: place the box upside down with the top flaps pointing outwards, so the opening faces the floor. As the cat may jump on the carrier, it should be sturdy enough to support her weight. In a different session, you can place the same carrier on its side or facing upwards.

However, there are a large number of other possible objects suited to the creativity training. Bags and backpacks are great, with their straps, lids and zips. You can also do a lot of things with boots or hiking shoes. A scrunched-up canvas shopping bag or a large stuffed animal also invites your cat to do all sorts of things. Remember one important criterion when you start out: you should choose an object which your cat is not familiar with on a day-to-day basis.

You will soon view your home with new eyes completely, checking all objects you have with regard to their suitability for clicker training – our cats aren't the only ones who will be stimulated to become more creative!

SET-UP
Let me describe the process of the '101-things-to-do' exercise using a shoulder bag as an example.

Begin the exercise in the same way as you did with the exercises performed so far: be observant of your cat's behaviour even before you place the shoulder bag in the vicinity of your cat, and be prepared with the clicker and titbits. Thus you will be able to use the clicker as soon as your cat looks at the bag. From then onwards click for everything – and I mean everything – that your cat offers you which is aimed in the direction of, or at, the bag. Initially, this includes any behaviour associated with movements towards the bag: looking at the bag, turning her head towards it, stretching her head forwards, getting up, signs of movement, one step or so determinedly in the direction of the bag, several steps…. It doesn't matter at all if you use the clicker when the cat moves towards the bag just by chance. After all, the sound of the clicker is the first indication for your cat that any actions regarding the bag are worth doing.

Once your cat has reached the bag, you can click and reward her for: stretching her head close to the bag; stretching her head close to its strap; sniffing one side of the bag; sniffing at the other side of the bag; playing with the zip; placing her left paw onto the front of the bag; stretching her left paw a little further towards the middle of the bag; placing her paw onto the left back side of the bag; pushing her left paw underneath the bag (the same also applies to her right paw, of course); placing her paw completely onto the bag; placing both front paws on the bag; the same process from the other side; squatting and looking into the bag; pushing one paw into the bag; pushing her head into the bag; climbing right into the bag; climbing back out of the bag; sitting next to the left side of bag; sitting next to the right of the bag; placing one paw underneath the shoulder strap; pulling on the shoulder strap; sniffing at the other zip; rubbing her head on the front corner; and rubbing her head on the back corner of the bag – I think you know what I am talking about.

This exercise is particularly suited for cats that are more passive by nature as well as for situations where things have gone wrong with the trick training as such. In both cases, easy and fast successes will give everybody involved in the training process renewed motivation.

In the event that your cat remains very passive, you should initially give her her titbit after the click a few cat-sized steps away. The cat will have to get up to receive her reward. Once your cat is standing, the next step will be that much easier. This, by the way, also applies to other tricks.

Use the clicker for every kind of behaviour your cat displays spontaneously. Don't use the clicker more than a maximum of twice in a row for one behaviour – after all, your cat should offer you different types of behaviour. Please accept the word 'different' in a very simple but very attentive sense: placing the paw an inch further up on an object is after all not exactly the same

101 things to do with a bag: left paw on the bag; right paw on the bag; both front paws on the bag; one paw on the bag; the other reaching further.
(Photos: Nissen)

One paw reaching over the bag; standing on the bag with both paws and sniffing at the centre of the bag; sitting on the bag with all four paws...
(Photos: Nissen)

movement as before. In this case, click and reward the differences your cat displays using her paws. For the cat, it is also a completely different mode of behaviour whether she uses the left or the right paw. From the point of view of the cat, the different sides of an object have an entirely different strategic value (aspects of camouflage and safety). That way, sitting in front of or behind the bag are different actions and therefore both deserve a click and reward. Your cat will soon realise that you do not expect her to do the same thing over and over again, but instead to vary her movements.

In the event that your cat doesn't find a lot to do with an object, or if this exercise is new for both of you, please use the clicker again for a kind of behaviour she has already shown you before. It ensures that the time lapse between two clicks doesn't become too long and prevents any possible frustration. Give your cat time to understand this new principle. Some cats understand it immediately; others only literally 'click' after a few 101-things-to-do training sessions. And that is perfectly OK.

Always end your training session while your cat is still alert and willing to learn. Do not ask for too much creativity in one go – that is a lot of fun, but it can be very exhausting, especially for more passive cats.

As far back as the 1960s, Karen Pryor described creativity exercises with the clicker. They were developed during training with dolphins, as a means to treat boredom and too much routine. The positive results were convincing and creativity exercises with objects have long and justifiably been incorporated into the usual range of clicker exercises.

(Photo: Nissen)

Ideas for tricks

Before you start teaching your cat one of the tricks described below, please always read the complete description first. In every case, contemplate whether a specific trick is suitable for your cat: is your cat active and agile or more laid-back and a bit sluggish? The former will have great fun jump-ing about and performing very active tricks. In the case of the latter, you should start getting your cat going with calmer tricks. Laid-back cats are usu-ally able to concentrate well, whereas fidgety ones don't (yet) have the ability to concentrate for long, which is necessary for more complex exercises.

Be creative

You don't need to teach one specific trick until your cat performs it perfectly before starting on the next one. On the contrary: cats revel in diversity and many get bored very quickly. Instead of repeatedly practising a single trick for the entire two-minute training session, practise two or three tricks within the same time span. Your cat will probably be even more willing to stay on the ball. It is important, however, that the tricks you are teaching within a training session are as diverse as possible in order not to confuse the cat. High five and sitting up, for example, are fairly similar, and you should avoid practising them at the same time. The same is true for lying down and rolling. On the other hand you can practise high five and lying down immediately after each other. In principle, active and passive exercises go very well together in one session.

There is no generally correct answer to the question of how long it will take for your cat to learn the individual tricks. Please do not push your cats too hard, and do not compare them to dogs. Some cats are highly motivated and have an incredibly fast acuity. With a well-designed overall training set-up they learn at an incredible speed. Other cats, on the other hand, follow the individual training stages in slow motion, and correspondingly require more time. That doesn't mean that they don't have the same fun or would profit any less from trick training. Speed is not important. The important factor is that you and your cat enjoy a nice experience together, spend active time with each other, have fun and hopefully learn something new – even about each other.

Is there anything within the exercise set-up that scares your cat? That is not the point and purpose of trick training. It is supposed to be fun, especially for your cat! Therefore, if a trick demands great strength of mind, put it right at the back for later. Once you have become an experienced trainer and your cat is an experienced and enthusiastic tricks cat, you can try that exercise again. You need to change the set-up of a potentially frightening exercise to ensure that your cat is only taxed to a slight stress level – anything else would be too much and would undermine good training. Split the trick into extremely small steps. Also, it should not be practised during each training session, and if you have practised it, always follow with one of your cat's favourite exercises or a huge reward. But, as I said, this is neither the time nor place for it.

You will soon discover what talents your cat has. There is nothing that says you cannot support these talents, and give your cat tasks which she can learn in play and without great exertion. The level of concentration needed during training is exhausting enough and successes are worth their weight in gold regarding self-esteem and feeling of well-being.

The exercise instructions in this book are not set in stone! There are always a number of ways to a goal, and one way may be more suitable for your cat than the one described here. By all means try out other well thought out and well planned techniques – sometimes diversions can turn out to be short-cuts.

ZsaZsi finds the balance exercise on the ball very exhausting. Make sure that your cat cannot injure herself performing this trick, by placing a cake tin underneath the ball to give it extra stability. Afterwards, follow with a very easy and relaxing exercise. (Photos: Nissen)

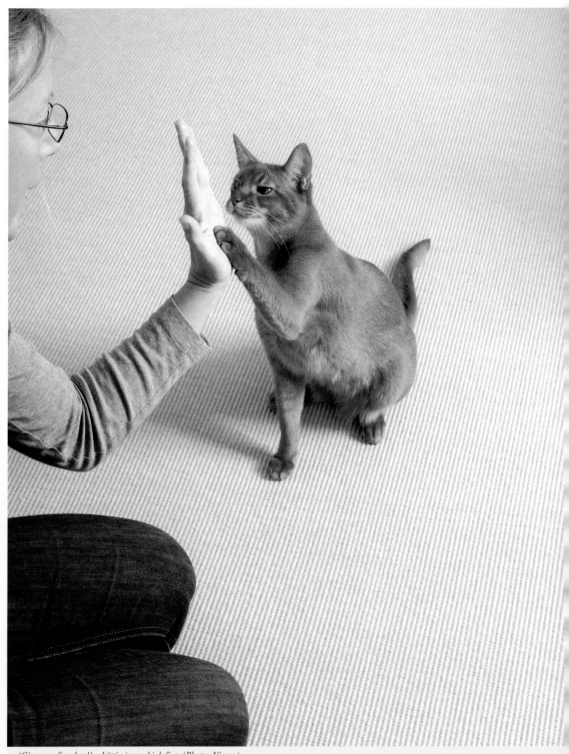

'Give us a five, bro!' – Lütti gives a high five. (Photo: Nissen)

Paw targets – example: High Five

For a high five: the cat places her paw in the centre of the upright palm of your hand. Paw target means: the cat touches a specific area of an object with her paw.

SET-UP

For high five hold up the palm of your hand towards your cat, at her approximate head height and at a length of more or less her front leg away. To begin with, click every approach towards your hand and shape every offer your cat gives you until she touches your hand with her paw. From now on your cat will only receive C & R for any physical contact with the paw. You can now shape the exercise, teaching your cat to touch the centre of the outstretched palm of your hand.

Possible steps:
• Looking
• A step towards the hand
• Sniffing
• Marking with her head
• Lifting paw
• Paw touches hand anywhere (probably on one side)
• Paw touches hand anywhere on palm of the hand
• Paw touches the centre of the palm of the hand

A variation of the high-five trick: if you hold the palm of your hand distinctly higher than his head, Eazy will give a high ten. (Photo: Nissen)

Note for rowdy cats

If your cat tends to use her claws, use shaping to teach her to place her paws softly on your hand. Once your cat touches your palm reliably, only allow her C & R when she offers the softly, softly touch; rough behaviour will not be rewarded.

Note for shy cats

If your cat feels threatened by your hand stretched up and out towards her, you can make things easier for her by introducing an interim step: don't hold your hand in the high-five position to begin with, but hold it palm upwards at the height of the cat's chest (as if you are offering her a titbit). Follow the shaping process as described above. Then turn your hand up and around in many small steps (and if necessary over several training sessions) and let your cat give you a number of high fives at every position. This helps her learn in a playful way that an upright hand in front of her face isn't actually a threat, but a promise of C & R.

Other targets for paw contact

You can teach your cat to touch a specific spot on all kinds of targets in the same manner. Initially, use the clicker for every approach and contact that your cat offers. Later, only reward her for touching the object with her paw, and eventually shape the trick so that your cat touches the desired spot.

ZsaZsi learns to place her front and hind paws in pairs on two different yoga blocks – for ZsaZsi, these are paw targets. As she still finds it a bit difficult to balance freely on all four paws, her trainer stabilises the upright block between her legs to ensure that nothing can go wrong. (Photos: Nissen)

Recognising colours

Under a variety of differently coloured nose or paw targets, your cat searches for the correct one. You will need targets that have the same shape, for example differently coloured beakers or table tennis balls on wooden skewers.

SET-UP
Now, use shaping to teach your cat to touch a nose target of a distinct colour (for example, white). Then use a target of the same construction but of a different colour (e.g. black) and place them both in front of your cat. Only let her have C & R if she touches the white target.

Once your cat touches the white target and ignores the black one, you can add individual targets in different and clearly recognisable colours/patterns (light/dark).

Variation for experienced cats
Connect touching the white target with the signal 'White'. In the same way but separately, shape touching the black target and linking it with the signal 'Black'. Ensure by way of frequent repetitions that your cat understands the differences. Now show her both targets at the same time and immediately make a colour signal – from now on your cat needs to touch the colour linked to the corresponding signal in order to get C & R.

If your cat finds this exercise easy to learn, increase the number of different colours.

Follow an exercise which requires physical effort with one that needs concentration: Eazy needs to touch the white target in order to be rewarded with C & R, irrespective of its position to the left, right, top or bottom of the black target. (Photo: Nissen)

Nose-to-nose kisses

Do you know the typical nose-to-nose greeting between cats? In this exercise your cat will give you a nose-to-nose kiss and at some stage may go to great lengths to do so.

SET-UP

Position yourself in such a way that your head and that of your cat are at the same level. Make sure that you are very comfortable so that you can easily maintain this position for a while. This is an exercise where you remain absolutely passive. You must not bring your head and nose forward and touch your cat. Instead the cat will have the active role. After all, she should not learn to receive the nose-to-nose contact but decide to initiate it on her own.

Stage 1

It depends entirely on your cat how much distance between the two of you is begun with and how many interim steps your cat needs. Pick it up where it is – literally: as soon as you are in the nose-to-nose position, use the clicker and reward the first movement of your cat towards you. Again, that may be a short glance, a slight turning of the head, or maybe even a few steps towards you. The reason is that we want to shape your cat on the way to your nose. If your cat moves towards you immediately, don't be too greedy and hope that she will reach your nose. Instead, use the clicker early so that even her first steps are rewarded. Otherwise, if your cat turns away before reaching your head, you will miss an important opportunity to use the clicker. Initially, give your cat her titbit in such a way that she can easily collect her next success by turning towards you again (look, turn of her head, turn of her body).

If your cat approaches you very hesitantly or moves about nervously at a certain distance from you, she is obviously rather wary of coming close to your head. You can make the exercise easier for her by not looking at her directly, but instead by turning your head slightly towards her, observe her out of the corner of your eye, blink frequently, and reward each look and each turning of the head towards you. Try to C & R your cat four or five times in the shortest time

The most convenient way to do clicker training with your cat is by sitting or kneeling on the floor. In that position, you generally have a lot of space, are approximately the same height as your cat and on what is a familiar habitat for her. If you have problems with your knees or back, or if you do not want to sit on the floor for any other reason, you can use a surface such as a large table for your trick training. In that case, you can stand or sit on chair in front of it and still remain close to your cat.

Faramir is already stretching quite far in order to reach his owner's nose. (Photo: Boumala)

possible and then end the training session or change over to another trick which your cat finds easier to do.

Stage 2

At this stage, your cat should walk up to your head regularly and speedily, as soon as you hold it in position. It would be typical cat behaviour if she were to kiss you directly on the nose as soon as she reaches you – use the clicker and give her the reward at a slight distance. Repeat this a few times so that your cat takes a few steps and then comes nose-to-nose with you.

In the event that your cat is too aggressive and almost breaks your nose, please try to grit your teeth a few times so that your cat can learn that she is on the right path. Be aware that your cat has just given you the gift of extremely friendly cat behaviour. As always, follow this with the shaping method and click and reward your cat for the slightly gentler kisses, while the roughest knocks do not result in C & R. As usual, during this shaping session, think of the importance of a high success rate for your cat and the small steps – this is the only way your cat can understand that you value gentle kisses.

If your cat is rather the opposite of aggressive and not very fast, simply continue shaping the last bit towards your nose. In this case, your cat is probably sitting at a small distance from you, or moves back and forth close to you. Use the clicker if she approaches your face a tiny bit. To begin with, this can by all means be your ear, your chin or your forehead. If the cat is moving about, increasingly shape any contacts in the direction of the nose. If she is sitting down, click and reward every slightest stretching in the direction of your nose. If you have long hair pull a few strands in front of your face – some cats find these easier to touch. Allow your cat plenty of time, over the period of many training sessions, to move closer and closer to the centre of your face and thereby your nose.

You could define the training goal as being that of your cat blowing gently at your nose from a distance of one centimetre. If a reserved cat does this while feeling perfectly fine, this is a sweet, touching exercise and a great effort on the part of your cat!

As a result of many repetitions, your position itself will become the signal for nose-to-nose. If you want to, you can now also introduce a verbal signal as soon as your cat reliably gives you nose-to-nose kisses: for example say 'kisses' and immediately get into the right position. Thus 'kisses' becomes an announcement of the 'nose-to-nose opportunity'.

All tricks that include physical contact with the cat should feel pleasant for her and smell nice. Choose clothing which the cat won't easily get her paws caught in and that feels pleasant under her paws, and avoid perfume and skin cream with a strong odour.

Stage 3

Once your cat gives you nose-to-nose kisses as soon as you get into position, follow up with the ultimate degree of difficulty: increase the distance. In the beginning remain on the same level as the cat and simply squat in front of her a bit further back. Then – still visible – position yourself behind or next to a chair, so the cat needs to overcome a small diversion. Hold your nose slightly higher so that your cat needs to stretch in order to be able to go nose-to-nose. Increase this until your cat needs to do a sit pretty to reach you or even has to jump on a chair or a table. Pulling or climbing up your clothes is only recommended for laid-back cats and when wearing suitable protective clothing.

As always, the principal rule is: only ever increase one criterion at a time.

After several training sessions Farimir even mounts a climbing drum for his nose-to-nose. (Photo: Boumala)

Pet carrier: cats on tour

Stage 1: The cat enters the open pet carrier willingly and perfectly happily and sits or lies down inside it.

Stage 2: The cat stays in the pet carrier with the door open.

Stage 3: The cat remains in the carrier in a relaxed manner with the door closed.

Stage 4: The cat stays relaxed and accepts being carried around in the carrier.

SET-UP

Teaching the cat to walk into the pet carrier is carried out in the same way as the exercise 'Sit on the blanket' (see page 33). For this purpose, the open pet carrier is turned towards the cat or positioned at a slight slant. To begin with remove the door completely.

Stage 1:
The cat enters the carrier and sits down
Possible steps:
❖ The way to the carrier
  • Looking at the carrier
  • Turning the head towards the carrier
  • Stretching the head towards the carrier
  • Minimum degree of approach towards the carrier
  • Standing up in the direction of the carrier
  • A single step towards the carrier
  • Several steps
❖ Having arrived beside or behind the pet carrier:
  • Touching any part of the carrier with her nose
  • Rubbing against any part of the carrier

Eazy promptly enters the carrier on signal and sits down – click and reward. He remains in the carrier in order to claim further C & Rs, and does not leave it until he is given the respective hand signal. (Photos: Nissen)

- Touching any part of the carrier with her paw
- Shaping the actions displayed slowly in the direction of the opening: as the cat sits next to the pet carrier, touching it with her paw will only be rewarded with C & R for any paw contact that is a little closer to the opening of the carrier than for paw contact elsewhere

❖ Having reached the opening of the carrier:
  - Nose or head anywhere on the opening
  - Paw anywhere on the edge of the carrier opening
  - Shaping the actions displayed so far

❖ Moving towards the centre of the respective edge of the carrier opening:
  - Looking inside the carrier
  - Sniffing inside the carrier
  - Stretching the head slightly
  - Stretching the head into the carrier another millimetre
  - Placing a paw inside the carrier
  - Placing two or three paws into the carrier

❖ Four paws inside the carrier:
  - When the cat first places her fourth paw into the pet carrier, give her a huge reward while she is still inside the carrier! When she has just finished eating her titbit, use the clicker again and give her another normal reward outside the carrier
  - Every now and then, preferably at the end of a training session, give your cat a large or great reward which she doesn't expect, whenever she has entered the carrier completely

❖ Sitting or lying down inside the carrier:
  - Delay the click once your cat has placed her fourth paw into the carrier. She will probably sit or perch down inside the carrier to wait – that is the moment for C & R!

The current status of the exercise would thereby be: cat sees the carrier, walks towards it and walks inside fully relaxed, turns around and sits or lies down. This stage should be repeated frequently, as well as the individual interim steps towards this goal.

Stage 2:
The cat remains inside the carrier with its door open
- Use the clicker if she sits/lies down in the carrier – give her the reward inside the carrier.
- Once your cat has finished her titbit, wait for a moment and then repeat C & R in the carrier.
- Repeat this step a few times.
- Increase the length of time that the cat lies down inside the carrier or finishes her titbit between the last click and the following one in steps of a second.
- If your cat has already reached the thirty-second interval, click and reward the cat at variable times – in other words, do not make it more difficult for her every time!
- Add a diversion: change your position and body posture, touch the carrier in different areas, allow other people or cats to be present, switch on the TV, sing a song … do not forget to initially reduce the length of time your cat is required to execute the exercise when introducing any diversion!

Stage 3:

The cat remains in the carrier in a relaxed manner with the door closed

By now, your cat should be quite relaxed inside the pet carrier, because it has revealed itself as a pleasant and rewarding place to be in the previous training sessions. However, from the point of view of the cat, an open pet carrier can be quite another kettle of fish to a closed pet carrier – after all, who wants to be locked in? Take great care and use sensitivity when you teach your cat to remain in the closed carrier. Also ensure that the door cannot close by accident.

Possible steps:
• Hooking the door in place
• Renewed shaping the approach to the carrier
• Renewed shaping of entering the carrier
• Renewed shaping of the cat remaining inside the carrier with a wide-open door

Now the cat is inside the carrier with the door wide open.
• Touch the door with your hand without closing it.
• Close the door around one centimetre and click. Open the door fully and give the titbit inside the carrier.
• Continue to close the door in tiny steps by repeating this process over and over.
• Leave the door in the closed position (but do not lock or clip it shut), open the door and reward your cat.
• Increase the length of time that the cat remains behind the shut but not locked door. Feed titbits through the holes in the door.

• Lock the door – click at the same moment as the noise of locking the door sounds and reward your cat inside the carrier. Then open the door immediately.
• Increase the length of time your cat remains in the completely locked pet carrier and give lots of C & R.

Stage 4:

Lift-off – the cat stays relaxed and accepts being carried around in the carrier

Possible steps:
• Touch the handle of the carrier
• Rattle the handle slightly

Diversions are fun! Eazy now likes to jump into his pet carrier and be carried around in it. (Photos: Nissen)

- Lift the pet carrier two centimetres, click and reward
- Lift the pet carrier five centimetres
- Increase the time the carrier is in the air, bit by bit
- Lift the pet carrier higher and higher up
- Don't just move the transport vertically but also sideways
- Take one step holding the carrier in your hand
- Walk several steps with the carrier in your hand
- Go into another room
- Go into a third room
- Add diversions
- Exit the front door of the home

There are cats that initially may prefer 'flying' with an open carrier door. Naturally, for when they need to be transported to the vet sometime in the future, they need to learn to be transported with a locked door as well.

During pet carrier training, be aware of your own posture, to ensure that you won't end up with backache!

Once your cat has learned to enjoy getting into the carrier, start placing the carrier in different locations. Place it a bit further away, then just around a corner, on the sofa, on the table, so that your cat must walk a longer distance, or even has to jump into it. Naturally, the pet carrier needs to be secured firmly for this exercise.

If your cat is afraid of the pet carrier, don't start this exercise until your cat has got a comprehensive positive clicker experience, and proceed extremely slowly and carefully. Observe the body language of your cat and do not overburden her. Under no circumstances should you entice your cat into the carrier with food – your cat needs to take every tiny step voluntarily and freely. This is the only way she will be able to overcome any possible fear.

Weaving in and out of your legs

Your cat weaves in and out of your legs while you are walking around. You can accomplish this through shaping, but as an alternative you can also help your cat understand by using the finger target.

SET-UP
In order to ensure that your cat can weave in and out of your legs smoothly, she always needs to weave through the legs from the position beside your back leg. That way, your back leg can take the next step without the cat being in the way.

Stage 1
You are standing in a walking position.
Possible steps:
- The cat looks through the legs
- First sign of approaching towards your legs
- All movements of walking in the direction of inside of your legs
- Touching the legs with head/body

• Touching the insides of your legs
• Weaving through the legs

After the click, always reward your cat in the direction of the movement through the legs, thus placing your cat in a favourable starting position again.

Stage 2
Start by standing with your legs in a walking position. If the cat has walked between your legs, take a step forward and stop again to enable your cat to do the same from the other side. After each successful traversing between the legs with C & R, take another step forwards.

Weaving through your legs during training: ZsaZsi weaves her way through the legs rubbing and smooching them. After the third step of the trainer she gets her well-earned click and reward. (Photos: Nissen)

Stage 3

Once stage 2 is working reliably, increase the requirements/demands: now your cat needs to weave in and out of the legs twice to earn her C & R. Then increase to three steps, four steps, and so on. Don't forget to make things easier for your cat every now and then.

Stage 4

Increase the walking speed until you can walk at your normal speed with the cat weaving in and out of your legs. (During this training exercise, reduce the number of steps your cat needs to take to be rewarded by C & R.)

Front paws on lower arm

The cat stands on her hind legs and places both front paws on your lower arm. You teach this exercise through shaping.

SET-UP

Hold your lower arm in a horizontal position slightly higher than the height of your cat's head – not above the head but instead approximately half an arm's length in front of it.

Possible steps:
• Looking at the arm
• Stretching the neck
• Touching/rubbing against the arm with head
• Touching the arm with her paw
• Sitting up in front of the arm
• Touching the arm and putting weight onto the arm

The horizontally positioned lower arm is the signal for Eazy to place his paws onto the arm. For the once very shy cat, this required a huge amount of conscious effort to begin with. (Photo: Nissen)

- Both front paws on the arm while 'sitting' on her hind legs
- Both front paws on the arm while standing on her stretched hind legs

Jumping through a hoop

Your cat jumps through a hoop held in position. The training technique for this exercise is shaping. Initially, the diameter of the hoop should measure at least 25 to 40 centimetres. At a later stage, you can decrease the size as a variation of the exercise. The smaller the hoop, the better you need to assess the natural jump curve of the cat and place the hoop in the correct position.

SET-UP

Stage 1
Hold the hoop approximately one hand's width above the floor with the outside edge touching a wall or a piece of furniture. You don't want your cat to run underneath the hoop or past it on the opposite side of where you are, and this will give her a greater chance of success.

Now click every approach your cat makes towards the hoop and then shape all her activities from the outer to the inner side of the hoop, and if possible towards the centre of the hoop. Then choose the activities where any body parts of your cat move a bit further through the hoop than usual – C & R. As soon as she sticks her head

The index finger of the hand holding the clicker shows Faramir the signal to jump through the hoop. (Photo: Boumala)

Clicker-pro Faramir jumps boldly through the hoop, the opening of which has been masked with a paper napkin. This exercise requires a very well planned and careful training routine. (Photo: Boumala)

through the hoop or stretches a paw through it, you can give the reward after the click on the other side of the hoop so that the cat passes completely through the hoop. This will help her to understand that she is supposed to pass through the hoop. Increase the demands until your cat walks through the hoop.

Stage 2
Hold the hoop a few centimetres higher so that your cat needs to jump through it. Increase the height bit by bit.

Tip: now include the jump through the hoop in exercises that require jumping that you have already taught your cat. For example, hold the hoop above an obstacle and only use the clicker when your cat jumps through the hoop. Many cats find this trick very easy to do.

For experienced cats and trainers: jumping through a hoop masked by a napkin
Depending on the selected hoop, you will need to choose different fixings for the napkin (for example, small pieces of Sellotape). An embroidery hoop allows the napkin to be secured tautly.

Possible steps:
• Fix one corner of the napkin at the top of the hoop.
• Fix the napkin loosely with two corners.
• Fix two napkins loosely in such a way the cat can see through an opening in the centre and can jump without too much resistance.
• Decrease the size of the opening in the centre.
• Secure one napkin to the hoop and cut a cross-section in the centre so that the cat can get through.

Preparation for the jump from chair to chair: Plato is given C & R for walking from one chair to the other.

Now the distance between the chairs is wide enough that Plato needs to make a very small jump or a very long step – however not so wide that the cat thinks walking on the floor is the easier option. (Photos: Boumala)

Jumping pro at work: Plato takes off fearlessly – click! – and lands safely on the other chair where he gets his reward. (Photos: Boumala)

• Decrease the size of the cross-section step by step
• Secure the napkin to the hoop and wet it slightly in the centre so that the napkin gives way at the slightest pressure.

Jumping between chairs

The cat jumps from one chair to another, which is placed at a correct distance for the cat to land on. Shaping is a suitable training technique.

SET-UP

Stage 1
Place two chairs directly next to each other so that the seats almost touch each other. Place your cat on one of the chairs by using the finger target.

Possible steps:
• Looking at the second chair
• Movement impulse towards the second chair
• First/second/third paw on the second chair
• Entire cat on the second chair

In this manner, let your cat move repeatedly from one chair to the other.

Stage 2
Increase the distance between the chairs, centimetre by centimetre. To begin with, the cat only needs to take longer strides to get onto the other chair – at some stage the cat needs to take her first small jump. Make sure that both chairs are positioned firmly during jump-off and landing.

Cuno follows a finger target over an extremely narrow plank of wood, which has been secured safely to the chairs with G-clamps. (Photo: Nissen)

Balancing act

The cat walks along a narrow plank over an 'abyss' between two chairs. She learns this exercise through shaping.

SET-UP

Depending on the agility of your cat, choose a plank that has a width of between 5 and 20 centimetres. Place each end on a chair in such a manner that it cannot tip up or fall down when the cat is walking on it. Small G-clamps may be of help.

Place your cat on one of the chairs with the help of a finger target, and shape the balancing act over the plank of wood.

Possible steps:
- Looking towards the other side
- Signs of moving in the direction of the second chair
- One/two/three/four paws on the plank
- One/two/three/several steps on the plank
- Complete traverse of the plank

Down

The cat lies down on her side or in the typical down posture – however, you should decide which position you want your cat to take. Capturing or enticing her with titbits are ways to achieve this goal.

SET-UP

It is relatively difficult to shape the down posture; it can however be captured very nicely during the day. Many cats lie down on their side after

Eazy has learned to lie down through capturing and now performs it on signal.

ZsaZsi has just been enticed to learn to lie down. Therefore, she is still intensely focused on the hand that gives the signal, even if the rewards are given with the other hand. (Photos: Nissen)

a prolonged play session – the perfect opportunity to give her C & R regularly. Of course, you can also utilise moments when your cat has just settled down on the window seat or the sofa. As soon as she is in the desired position – C & R. If, after a number of repetitions, you notice that your cat lies on her side with marked frequency, it is time to introduce a signal.

If you have a very calm and passive cat, there is a danger that she offers this trick to the exclusion of all others. Therefore it is not suitable as a first exercise to teach.

Later on, when you ask for the trick by signalling your cat, please take into account that it requires a certain degree of quiet and relaxation. It can be a good thing if your currently excited cat lies down on your signal – but it will be a very difficult thing for her to do!

Birne runs purposefully through the tunnel – click! – and is then given his reward. (Photo: Nissen)

If you have a very gentle cat – then, but only then – you can also use food to entice your cat to lie down. Place a titbit between your thumb and your outstretched hand in such a manner that the titbit is on the palm side of your hand. Show it to your cat and then slowly move your hand on the floor away from the cat. Click and reward the cat for crouching down and moving her head close to the floor in order to be able to push her mouth underneath your hand. With time, become ever more demanding until you only give C & R once your cat lies flat on the ground with her front legs stretched out forwards. Don't forget, the movement with your hand will be sufficient after just a few repetitions – it is the signal for 'down'.

Lütti proves with his focused jump that tunnels also make excellent obstacles. (Photo: Nissen)

Through a tunnel

Your cat runs through a tunnel without hesitating. The most suitable object for this trick is a tunnel made of nylon with stable sides. The method used to teach your cat this trick is shaping.

SET-UP
Lay the tunnel next to a wall or a piece of furniture. Shape all movements that your cat makes towards the opening of the tunnel:

- Looking in the direction of the tunnel
- Approach
- Sniffing at the tunnel
- Marking the tunnel from the outside with her head
- Marking the tunnel on the inner edge
- Looking into the tunnel
- Kneading
- Placing one paw inside

As soon as your cat has all four paws in the tunnel, use the clicker and reward her without delay at the other end of the tunnel.

Obstacle course

Your cat jumps or otherwise overcomes a course of several obstacles – chairs, obstacles, tunnel, balancing act and so on.

SET-UP
Use any kind of obstacles for a small agility course, which you have already used for individual exercises. It is easier if your cat already knows the individual obstacles. If you want to combine them into a course, please proceed as follows.

- Always place your cat's favourite obstacle, or one that it knows particularly well and

Eazy overcomes a small course which ends with his favourite obstacle, the drum – click! (Photos: Nissen)

overcomes without hesitation, as the last one in the course.

• In front of that erect a second obstacle. Your cat needs to master this one before she is allowed to jump over her favourite one.

• Initially help your cat with the finger target to give her a hint that you expect her to do a different exercise from usual, namely overcome the last obstacle. Only use the clicker at the precise moment at which your cat jumps over the last obstacle.

• Once your cat traverses both obstacles safely, add a third jump as the new first obstacle of the course.

Please take care to ensure that the distances between the obstacles are neither too short nor too long and that all obstacles are placed securely. Use outer boundaries such as walls or wardrobes to help your cat steer correctly over the course.

101 Movements

In this exercise the cat creatively shows different movements and positions of her body, which are clicked and rewarded. As in the 101-things exercise, there is no fixed goal. The different actions on part of the cat are captured during the exercise (capturing).

101 movements: Plato offers different movements one after the other – turning of his head to the right, lying down, stretching the right paw forwards, a turn to the right and a look to the left. If you have a novice cat, the movements can naturally be less pronounced. (Photos: Boumala)

SET-UP

This is a variation of the 101-things exercise, however without an object and therefore more difficult for the cat to do. Click and reward your cat for each slightest movement and each smallest change in posture: sitting down, getting up, turning her head to the left/right, turning the head further, lying down on her tummy, lying down on her side, lifting one paw slightly, lifting one paw slightly higher, lifting up the other paw slightly, making a turn, crossing over her paws, lifting/pressing down her head, sitting up and so on.

The goal is for your cat to display as many different movements as possible and for you not to click the same movements repeatedly, but only each different movement. Initially, however, you do not have to be as strict.

If you lay down a specific cloth for your cat during this exercise, it will soon become the 'be creative' signal for your cat. Clearing away the cloth subsequently shows the cat that the session is over.

Other ideas for tricks

Just to make sure that you don't run out of ideas too quickly, the following are some suggestions for tricks that your and your cat can work out together.

The following tricks are especially suited for training the cat through shaping:

• Jumping onto/over your bent leg
• Jumping through your arms
• Jumping onto your arm
• Walking to heel
• Balancing on a gymnastics ball
• Jumping onto your lap
• Turning around in a circle
• Running around two obstacles in a figure of eight
• Go fetch!
• Ringing a little bell
• Crawling
• Waving

You can capture the following tricks during the day or during a training session (capturing):

• Sit!
• Yawning
• Bowing (front down, backside up)
• Spanish step (stretching her front leg straight forward)
• Stretching her hind leg straight back
• Arching her back
• Standing still
• Special movements or actions which the cat demonstrates during play/hunting
• Meowing on signal order
• Eye contact

This requires balance and closeness: Birne climbs onto the shoulder of a person he is not familiar with in a series of shaping steps. This exercise is easier if another person with an unrestricted view of the cat takes over the clicking. (Photos: Nissen)

(Photo: Rüter)

Trick training with several cats

Teaching tricks with several cats at the same time is a matter for professionals. Initially, you should always train each cat on her own, to ensure that you are able to concentrate completely and fully on that cat. Cats also find it easier to understand the clicker principle and to learn new tricks if they are not distracted by other cats and confused by 'strange clicks' meant for other cats.

Excursion into door training

Does your cat not really like closed doors? In this case, start by carrying out the following door training exercise together.

STAGE 1

Start the door training during normal daily situations. Close a door, throw a titbit down for your cat and then immediately open the door again. After a number of repetitions, the cat will connect the closing of the door with a positive action.

However, if your cat starts to panic seriously even if the door is only shut for a second and is unable to eat its titbit, you should not continue – you may need to seek professional help.

STAGE 2

Delay the opening of the door for a moment or so. Does your cat miaow or scratch at the door? Wait until it displays the first moment of calm or the first movement away from the door – and then open the door. Your cat will learn through repetitions that calm behaviour opens the door but that making a fuss, on the other hand, won't open it.

STAGE 3

Extend, in many small steps, the length of time your cat needs to stay calmly in front of the closed door until it opens again. As soon as you have reached a time span of one or two minutes, you can carry out short clicker sessions on the other side of the door. Sweeten the length of time your cat is expected to wait with a fun/activity board for cats.

This trick requires a lot of practice and prolonged concentration for it to work in as relaxed a way as shown here: during the exercise Cuno and Lütti receive titbits to reward them for calmly remaining in their place waiting, while Birne performs active tricks. (Photo: Nissen)

Clicker training with several cats at the same time

To begin with, you need to have taught your cats in individual previous training sessions to stay put on a place mat or in the pet carrier. Now you can demand these exact exercises in joint training sessions. Let the first cat go into the pet carrier and make sure she remains there. Now – depending on the degree of training – you have a few seconds up to a few minutes to be able to concentrate on the second cat. During this time, you need to give the cat who is waiting titbits at irregular intervals. As waiting is far more difficult if another cat is present who is moving around and receiving rewards, you will initially need to increase the number of titbits when you are training more than one cat at a time. In

Cats who are at an advanced training level and who are very familiar with each other: given the right signal, Farimir jumps over Plato's back who, at the same time, touches the target hand with his nose. Naturally, you will first need to teach each cat the signal to jump over an obstacle and the nose target intensively, during individual training sessions. (Photo: Boumala)

addition, don't forget to switch the roles of the active and the waiting cat at regular intervals. Find out whether your cats prefer to wait a little longer and subsequently have more time in active training, or whether it works out better for them if you change from one cat to another every minute or so.

Studying joint tricks with several cats

The following are initial suggestions for tricks with at least two cats. Decide whether your cats get along well enough with each other to learn these tricks together, without the atmosphere becoming strained or a cat becoming scared. If your cats tend to keep apart during the normal daily routine, don't overtax them with a trick which requires close contact. Observe in particular whether all cats that are taking part during joint training sessions are feeling well.

Jumping over another cat

A cat jumps over another cat. During this trick the cat who plays the role of the obstacle is contained in a secure container, for example in a tunnel, a little cardboard house, or a pet carrier.

The cat that does the jumping should not jump onto the container, if possible. If she does so anyway, the container needs to be strong enough to ensure the safety of the cat within! Using a hoop held above the container may encourage the cat to actually jump clear over the container.

SET-UP

The cat who is taking the role of the passive partner has already learned to wait, for example in the tunnel, for a period of at least 30 seconds. Ask her to get into the tunnel and sit down. Now give the 'active' cat the signal to jump over the tunnel. If she hesitates, use the clicker for signs of an approach as you would with any new obstacle. Both cats get their earned reward for every click.

If both cats are able to wait and jump, let them change roles in the next training session.

Nose-to-nose

The cats touch each other with their noses – a trick you teach with the capturing technique.

SET-UP

Keep your eyes open and the clicker in your hand at all times and give your cats C & R if they greet each other nose-to-nose during the day. You need to make absolutely sure that you really use the clicker at the precise moment when their noses are almost touching each other – and not when they are already moving away from each other. If your cats now begin to show nose-to-nose in all kinds of situations where they are not actually greeting each other, it is time to introduce a signal, for example a verbal 'Kitty-Kiss!'

This exercise can support the friendly contact between your cats. However, if your cats never greet each other in this manner, you need to be extra careful if you want to reach this extremely close contact through shaping, for example. There is a high risk that you will intrude upon the private space of one of your cats during this exercise. In that case, think of a different exercise which respects the requirements of your cats. Maybe they can each sit on either armrest of a sofa at the same time? Or they could balance across parallel wooden planks? Or sit in two pet carriers next to each other?

You can capture any friendly nose-to-nose greetings between your cats with the clicker and shape a trick out of this behaviour. (Photo: Boumala)

Epilogue

Whenever you and your cat are doing clicker training, please don't forget the following: it is completely unnecessary that the final result looks great and spectacular. The path leading up to the completed trick is far more important for me because it is quality time I have spent with my cat in a friendly, fun and exciting way. Once your cat is able to perform the tricks laid out in this book, both of you will have learned and performed a lot of things.

But if you are interested in more, this is just the beginning. Devise your own new tricks. Observe your cat and offer her exercises which emphasise her individual talents. Dare to change the exercises that are suggested in this book in a way which simply works better for your cat and yourself. If you encounter difficulties, go back through the book and reread the general paragraphs regarding the make-up of the training sessions. You will find that the importance of many details only becomes clear once you have started with the practical work.

Read everything you can get your hands on regarding clicker training with cats, whether in books or on the Internet. Try finding other like-minded people with whom you can exchange ideas and experiences. Books regarding clicker training with dogs or horses also include a number of exercises which can be adapted to be used for cats.

Utilise every opportunity to use clicking, not just with your own but also with other cats, and to gain more experience. Ask your local animal sanctuary whether they will allow you to brighten up the daily routine of the cats living there.

I wish you and your cat(s) much fun during your trick training!

Further Reading

Books

Braun, Martina,
Chat to Your Cat:
Lessons in Cat Conversation. Cadmos, 2009.

Braun, Martina,
Clicker Training for Clever Cats.
Cadmos, 2009.

Dbalý, Helena/Sigl, Stefanie,
Playtime for Cats: Activities and
Games for Felines.
Cadmos, 2009.

Fields-Babineau, Miriam,
Cat Training in 10 Minutes.
TFH Publications, 2003.

Hauschild, Christine,
No Love for the Litter Box?
Understanding and curing house-soiling in cats.
Books on Demand, 2010.

Moore, Arden,
Teaching Your Cat Simple Tricks.
Storey Books, 2000.

Parsons, Emma,
Click to Calm.
Sunshine Books Inc., 2004.

Pryor, Karen, Clicker Training for Cats.
Waltham, MA: Sunshine Books, 2001.

Pryor, Karen,
Reaching the Animal Mind.
Ringpress Books, 2002.

Internet

www.pets.groups.yahoo.com/group/Cat-Clicker

Contact the author

Christine Hauschild
Mobile Katzenschule Happy Miez
(Mobile Cat School: Happy Kitty)
www.mobile-katzenschule.de/english.html

Index

CADMOS Cats

Helena Dbalý/Stefanie Sigl
Playtime for cats

Great ideas for spicing up your cat's play! Playtime for cats is very important. Cats need to play in order to safeguard their well-being and physical and mental fitness, and to prevent the development of behavioural abnormalities. The book offers a whole host of creative ideas, guaranteeing lots of excitement and fun for humans and cats of any age!

112 pages, full colour, Softcover
ISBN 978-3-86127-970-9

Martina Braun
Chat to your cat

Cat language is both complex and multifaceted: cats do so much more than just miaow, hiss and purr! Find out what your little tiger is really saying with all his many different sounds, facial expressions, body posture and little behavioural quirks. Once you understand your cat better, you can get to grips with some of the typical problems and develop a closer bond to your moggy.

80 pages, full colour, Softcover
ISBN 978-3-86127-966-2

Martina Braun
Clicker Training for clever cats

Classical conditioning, used in a specific way in clicker training, is a method of learning, which no mammal is impervious to – not even the cat. Every click results in a positive reward: a treat, a cuddle, a favourite game. And because cats are intelligent, they quickly understand what kind of behaviour gets them a reward. This book gives you the chance to explore a new world together with your cat, from teaching small tricks to commands.

80 pages, full colour, Softcover
ISBN 978-3-86127-967-9

For more information, please visit:
www.cadmos.co.uk

CADMOS